The Busy Mom's Greatest Companion

The Busy Mom's Greatest Companion

Your Guide to Going from Overwhelmed to Overjoyed

Tracy E. Munson

Natural Health Strategist, NHP, CDC

Editorial: Shirarose Wilensky
Cover Design & Illustration: Natalie Gower
Author Photo: Rozalind Ewashina Photography

ISBN-13: 978-0-9951889-0-7
ISBN-10: 0995188904

Printed in CANADA

***

To my husband, Owen, and children, Mackenzie,

Anisty, Corvin, & Ella.

"Do you know what?"

***

"YOU LOVE ME!!"

It is true....

I love you, more than you will ever know.

Contents

Preface

From Overwhelmed to Overjoyed

I would like to share my story with you, not for sympathy or judgment but to demonstrate that no matter how low you feel, there is always a light shining at the end of the tunnel.

I was born in New Westminster, British Columbia. While growing up, I was faced with situations that have made me who I am today. School was a challenge, and I quickly learned that when I asked for help, I would be turned down or redirected. Since I started off in a very large, very busy K–12 school, it was easy for me to slip through the cracks. I remember in Grade 2, during reading time, I went to the shelf and grabbed a small chapter book. I read all the words that I knew—"the," "a," "and"—and then put the book back on the shelf. My teacher asked, "You're done already?" and I nodded. At this point, I knew something wasn't right, as all the other kids were reading these books. At lunch one day, I asked my teacher for help. She said to talk to the librarian. He said, "That isn't my job. Go to your teacher." I didn't ask anyone else for help in fear of rejection.

Later that year, my family moved to Whitecroft, a small village near Sun Peaks Resort, north of Kamloops,

B.C. I was angry at my parents for making me move, and sad to leave my friends, our house, what was familiar and my half brothers, who lived with their other parents, but the change truly was a blessing and a gift. At my new school, the teachers realized that I was behind on my reading and put me into an extra program to allow me to catch up.

Rejection and the disappointment of others kept coming up throughout my life, from friends and family to coaches and complete strangers. Throughout my childhood and adolescence, I don't remember getting much praise for doing my best. I was involved in different sports growing up. When I was first starting out, I remember being so excited and happy just to be playing, but it only took a couple of games where I was criticized at the end for what I did wrong, without receiving any praise to go along with it, for me to get discouraged. I can remember one soccer game in particular: I was playing left defense, which is in the last line, right before the goal. A player from the opposing team was making a breakaway towards me, but I was able to steal the ball and start on a breakaway of my own. Somehow, I was able to deke and fake players out, making it to the goal for a shot at net and scoring my very first goal. Later in the same game, I was playing a little higher up the field than I should have been, which allowed an opposing player to go on a breakaway and score a goal. After the game, the parent I was carpooling with said nothing about the goal I had scored but focused solely on the mistake I had made—if only I had been where I should have been, that goal against us would never have happened. The negative, or what I could have done better, was always the focus, rarely what I had done well. I became very hard on myself and soon couldn't see that I did anything right. Failure and mistakes were so programmed within me as bad things that I completely feared them.

I had to grow up quicker than most of my peers. My parents always provided for me, but if I wanted anything "extra," I had to work for it myself. I started babysitting when I was nine and got my first real job when I was thirteen, as a janitor, to pay for the extra sports fees and equipment I needed and clothes that my parents couldn't afford. Throughout high school, I always had at least two jobs; plus, I volunteered at a local martial arts school, teaching and training in the hope that one day I would get a paid position. Having two jobs ended up conflicting with why I was working in the first place. I was working to be able to pay to play basketball and represent Kamloops in soccer around the province, but I often had to miss basketball practice because I had to work. My coach lectured me, saying I should enjoy my high school years and basketball; I had the rest of my life to work. What he didn't understand was that if I wanted to play, I had to work. Between the extra pressure from my coach and juggling my work and sports schedules , I was so overwhelmed that I ended up having to forfeit my position on the basketball team. I was miserable, because I was working my butt off to do what I wanted but just ended up being a disappointment to the people around me. This resulted in me accepting more shifts and working my way out of school, graduating six months early.

One day, I noticed an ad in a newspaper for the Canadian Institute of Natural Health and Healing. I was instantly interested. I have always been intrigued by the healing arts and natural health, so when I graduated from high school, I got a full-time job and was saving money to go to this college to become a natural health practitioner. Fourteen months later, I graduated and received my diploma in natural health and healing, but I had already decided that I was changing my career path. While I was going to school, I got a lot of pushback from family members, who said my chosen field wasn't credible; it was hocus-pocus. They said, "You're not even a massage therapist or physiotherapist" and "You'll never succeed unless you get a real diploma." I decided to become an electrician instead, because I thought that would make my family happy. It did.

When I look back at going to school to become a natural health practitioner, I found it easy, it came to natural me and I loved it! When I went to school to become an electrician, it was very difficult and I had to work my butt off, which left me feeling stressed, frustrated and anxious. Even the mention of a test would send me into panic mode. In hindsight, I see that when you're on the right path, doing something you love, it comes with ease and enjoyment.

One of my childhood dreams was to get married and have a family. By nineteen I was engaged, and within six months I married my life partner. Again, I received a lot of pushback from family and friends. They said I was too young, my life would be over and I could say good-bye to my career as an electrician. This time, I followed my heart and pursued my dream. My husband and I planned to start a family right away, and I became pregnant shortly after our wedding. We were so excited, but the reaction I received from those close to me was, again: "I wish you had waited and gotten your career done." I had a miscarriage. This was devastating. My four pregnancies to follow inspired similar reactions: "This baby is too close to the last," "I thought you were done" and "I guess I'm happy for you." An extremely exciting time was turned into a disappointment or something that I was doing wrong.

After my third child was born, I remember having so many personally destructive emotions: I was miserable, overwhelmed, my marriage was failing and I was desperate to find "me." I didn't get it; I thought I had exactly what I wanted. I had a well-paying job, as an electrical lead hand/supervisor, clearing more than $110,000 a year. I had benefits and a pension plan. I was getting the praise I always wanted and had a family with three amazing children. I didn't know where to turn, so I went to the doctor. Instantly, as soon as I started to talk, tears welled in my eyes and started overflowing uncontrollably. I shared my thoughts through gasps of breath and blurry eyes: "I'm the biggest failure as a parent," "I am always yelling," "I feel so terrible for my children," "They deserve better," "They would be better off without me." These are just some of the terrible feelings I shared. If there were a color to symbolize how I was feeling, it would be the darkest black. The doctor said it was clear I was depressed; I should go on antidepressants and seek out a counselor. I agreed with the depression diagnosis, but I refused the antidepressants. I looked into counselors when I got home, but none of them felt right. After letting all my emotions out to my doctor, I felt better and thought I was fine and could handle things myself, so I brushed off his recommendations.

A year and a half later, I was still going down in my spiral of destruction. I was angry, frustrated and lashing out. I would become overwhelmed by the smallest tasks, felt stuck and alone, but I couldn't figure out why. I was pregnant with our fourth baby, and I was at the bottom, in my darkest moment. It got to the point where my husband said, "You really need to figure your stuff out because I can't do this anymore."

That evening, again, I searched for counselors in my area. This time, I found one, Leanne Oaten, who felt right just by reading her business name. She specializes in managing stress, addressing adrenal fatigue and empowering women to achieve vital health, fulfillment and success on all levels. Right away, without hesitation, I filled in a "contact me" form and, to my surprise, received a response that evening and booked my first appointment. With some amazing advice and support from her, I quickly realized I was on the wrong path both mentally and spiritually. Once I dug deep within myself, I found happiness in just the thought of going back to what I loved doing as a natural health practitioner. This realization allowed me to begin my journey to finding and healing me.

These life events have made me who I am and explain why I am so passionate about helping others. This is why I am a natural health strategist and mom's coach, specializing in assisting overwhelmed moms restore their calm and happiness, even through the busyness of life. It is easy to lose ourselves in a busy world full of social expectations and unrealistic beliefs about what makes a perfect life. My vision is for all moms to think of themselves as extraordinary! I love seeing my clients overcome their challenges, and it warms my heart to help them along the way. It is rewarding to witness the shifts that allow them to move forward and live happier lives.

Through my own personal journey—my life learnings and discoveries, my experiences and the training I have received—and those of my clients, I realized that I could reach so many more with a book. This book. I share my story in the hope that it can assist you in your own journey. I will be sharing some of my dark moments and how I was able to overcome them. Some of these moments will resonate with you, whereas others may not, or they may later on, as you overcome each challenge. Your journey is unique to you; let yourself process and progress at your own speed.

Some of my life experiences were painful at the time and are still raw now. Know that if I can go from deep darkness to happiness and love, from overwhelmed to overjoyed, so can you! Use these examples as a demonstration of what you can accomplish. Sometimes the low points in our life are there to build us stronger for the future, and sometimes they are there to redirect us onto a better path towards happiness and purpose. My advice to you is to be open to new perspectives, discoveries and ideas; remain patient with yourself; and keep in mind that breaking old habits and forming new ones takes time. Allow yourself to explore and find new things that make you happy, and do more of them.

There is no such thing as a straight path of motherhood. It's hard, it's imperfect and it's a process filled with discoveries and learning. In our society, we have been programmed to believe that if our life isn't perfect and easy, we're failing. A lot of people are so worried about what "everyone else" thinks, but really "everyone else" is busy focusing on themselves and what *they* are doing. And even if they aren't, it really doesn't matter what *they* think anyway. There is no such thing as a purely perfect and easy life. There are perfect and easy times, but often it takes some discoveries to get there. Life is full of ups and downs, tests and triumphs, mistakes and learning. And life is full of discoveries. It is all in the eye of the beholder.

I often share a quote by spiritualist Don Miguel Ruiz, one that may resonate with you: "The only person in control of my happiness and success is me."

Introduction

From Outward to Inward

This may not be an easy time in your life. Whatever has brought you to this book is your story and has made you who you are today. It is not uncommon for women to take on other people's "stuff": your children's, husband's, friends', colleagues'. It is also easy to put your own needs and feelings on the back burner. The never-ending daily tasks—to-do lists, work, children, finances, meals, chores—make it easy to keep too busy. Do you find yourself saying you're "too busy" to do something? Too busy to go out with your friends, too busy to do something you love—a favorite hobby or activity—too busy for time with your children or husband? It is not uncommon to feel lost, displaced and disconnected within your own skin. And adding the title "Mom" can increase these feelings tenfold. Being occupied by other people's needs each and every day without honoring your own can lead to exhaustion and deep disconnection.

Many women and mothers are not entirely sure who they truly are; they are detached from themselves. Living a life from an outward perspective, in a world full of judgment, with the accompanying pressure to portray a perfect life and self-imposed unrealistic expectations, can result in feelings of disappointment and failure. In our affluent Western society, we have essentially been programmed to put on a facade to express how "ideal" our life should be, how we should appear in the eyes of the general population. There is the accepted way to be, look, act; the right house, vehicle, life to strive for; the correct things to have. But really, all these things should be customized to each individual—who you are, your personality, what you like to do and what you want to accomplish in your life. Not everyone is the same. Each woman, each mom, will do things differently, have different beliefs and priorities, and have different techniques that work better for her. Thus the importance of focusing inward, rather than outward.

The Busy Mom's Greatest Companion is a book to assist you in finding the balance between life, work and you. Specific techniques will allow you to live your life with less stress, more stability and a greater sense of ease. Simple language and real-life scenarios and stories will provide you with the tools to reconnect you with the things that you enjoy, to honor yourself daily and to find love within you again. This book will help you release the judgments of others and honor yourself and what you love to do, truly connecting you with yourself and your desires. To heal your relationship with yourself and let go of judgments gives your children the best chance for a happy and healthy relationship with themselves in turn.

Every challenge is an opportunity to learn, grow and better yourself. *The Busy Mom's Greatest Companion* will help you see the learning and growth available in difficult situations. This will have positive effects and change your life drastically. When you're able to approach situations with a positive outlook, and accept any discoveries to learn and grow, you will not only better yourself but be a much happier person. You will be able to overcome many hurdles, just by connecting within, changing your mindset and becoming self-aware and self-observant, meaning that you're able to feel in your heart what is right for you and honor yourself in standing strong in your beliefs, knowing when something is "off" and redirecting your path to rectify it. Becoming more self-aware and self-observant will also allow you to notice when you're in error and correct yourself without penalizing yourself, moving forward with ease.

It is time to allow yourself to feel better, one step at a time. *The Busy Mom's Greatest Companion* will guide you on your journey to feeling happy, satisfied and confident in your decisions and personal growth. As your sense of self-connection increases, you will see and feel a vast difference in the ease with which you navigate your relationships and life's ups and downs. Your journey may not be easy, but every trial can lead to happiness, if you're willing to put the time in and work for it. At this moment, you may not feel or believe it's possible; however, allow yourself to be open to the possibility of being extraordinary. It is a journey worth taking. When you're ready, I recommend seeking support, as this journey should not be traveled alone. Find a counselor or mentor who is a good fit for you. Know that new mentors will come into your life at the right times as you grow and progress through your journey.

If you have a partner, I recommend being open and honest about your entire journey from the very start. This will increase their awareness and allow them to understand what you're going through and how you're feeling. Communication is an essential part of this journey; the more open you are in sharing your experiences with your partner, the more understanding they can be, the closer you will become and the easier conflicts will be to resolve and the less they will happen. Speak your truth and nourish your spirit. Being with someone who promotes growth and well-being in themselves and their partner by means of clear communication and empathetic understanding is the greatest gift for a relationship. Share with each other and assist each other in reaching your goals, both individual and collective.

My journey began because I was hurting my loved ones. I wanted to get better for them but quickly realized how good I felt when I started to look after myself. I wanted to continue to feel this way, not only for my loved ones but for me. With ongoing support from key mentors in my life, I continue to better myself. With the tools, techniques and practices found in this book, I am optimistic you will be able to do the same.

This is your journey; you be the guide. Take the first step to going from overwhelmed to overjoyed.

Tools to Enhance Your Progress

- Do your best to read this book every day. Revisit each chapter the following day (for example, Day 1—read Chapter 1, Day 2—reread Chapter 1, Day 3—read Chapter 2, and so on). This will allow you to really absorb the information, but of course you should do what feels right to you. Some chapters may need more time than others.

- Take notes or use a highlighter as you read to increase absorption. An added benefit is that if you revisit a chapter in a few months and use a different color highlighter, you will see your growth and the new discoveries you've made since the first time, and each time you reread this book.

Chapter 1

Reconnect with You

"Being a mother is learning about strengths you didn't know you had and dealing with fears you didn't know existed."

—Linda Wooten, Author of Mothers Thoughts

That moment when you feel so emotionally low that you can't imagine getting any lower, when you're so mad or frustrated with yourself that you mentally beat yourself up and punish yourself, or someone else—this is the starting point for most. The point when you realize you are unhappy and need something to change. This state is incredibly powerful and damaging on an intense level, which is why it is important to stop the flow of emotion at the beginning. Envision a tornado: the top is huge and wide, but it gradually gets smaller and darker as it gets closer to the ground. Stop the emotion as close to the top of the tornado as possible. The further you spiral down, the more difficult and detrimental it is to recover.

Are you feeling this way now, or have you recently? You are not alone. According to the World Health Organization (WHO), 350 million people suffer from depression around the world every year, yet we still don't talk openly about it. I can't know whether you're depressed but rather include this statistic to demonstrate the number of people suffering—and that is only the people who have come forward to ask for help. The Health Canada website states, "About 11% of men and 16% of women in Canada will experience major depression in the course of their lives. Depression can limit your quality of life, affect relationships, lead to lost time from work or school and contribute to other chronic diseases such as diabetes and heart diseases. Sometimes it leads to suicide. Fortunately, for most people, depression can be treated effectively."

However, people first need to know whether they suffer from depression and, above all, what it is. Without looking into what depression is, many people will deny that it is even a possible factor in how they feel.

The Public Health Agency of Canada lists the following symptoms of depression:

- Feeling guilt
- Helplessness or hopelessness
- Loss of interest in usual enjoyed activities
- Weight or appetite changes
- Fatigue or decreased energy
- Difficulty concentrating or making decisions
- Trouble sleeping

Depression doesn't have to be viewed as a bad thing; it is your body telling you that something is wrong, a message to reconnect. It may be that you're in a job you don't enjoy, you've been keeping yourself too busy and neglecting yourself or you have a chemical deficiency or hormonal imbalance within your body. Your state of mind may be out of your control. My advice is to seek support and visit a naturopath, family doctor, counselor, psychologist or psychiatrist. According to the Canadian Encyclopedia of Natural Medicine and Rocky Mountain Analytical, a Canadian saliva hormone testing lab, seven out of ten women who suffer from symptoms of depression have laboratory-confirmed hormonal imbalance. I highly recommend visiting a hormonal specialist to check your levels, as this is a very common issue for women that can be easily misdiagnosed. The good news is that hormonal imbalance, chemical deficiency and depression can all be treated and rectified. Here are just some of the signs and symptoms of hormonal changes and imbalance, from a very long list:

• Headaches/migraines	• Miscarriages
• Irritability	• Low Sex Drive
• Acne and pain	• Hair Loss

• Insomnia/poor Sleep	• PMS
• Brain Fog/memory Loss	• Hot Flashes
• Anxiety	• Fatigue
• Bloating	• Fibroids
• Heavy periods	• Ovarian Cysts
• Water retention	• Endometriosis
• Depression	• Fibrocystic breasts

As a mom, it can be easy to feel lost, displaced or disconnected. Becoming a mom changes your whole world, whether it be your first, second, third or fourth child (or more!). If you feel like you're struggling, don't hide it. My clients frequently bring up this issue, saying things like: "I should be able to handle it all by myself," "I don't want anyone to know I'm having a hard time keeping up," "I don't want them to tell anyone I'm failing." What drives a mom to this intense emotional state? Often it is a result of setting yourself up for failure by piling too much on your plate, not asking for help and trying to do it all. It can also be caused by feeling as though you have to be someone you're not in order to fit in, suppressing who you really are to be accepted. Often these fears are associated with family, friends and the social expectations of perfection, and the "weakness" of asking for help. So you put on a mask and pretend everything is okay, but deep down you're struggling. One of my clients was so afraid her friends and family would find out that she wasn't accomplishing all that she portrayed. She felt like such a failure because she couldn't keep up with her massive daily to-do lists, but she wouldn't ask for help. She thought, "I can't even keep up with my house and I only have one child!" I love the saying "It takes a village to raise a child," because you are not meant to do it on your own. And those who care about you will want to do what they can to assist you.

The expectations that we have learned to meet in order to be accepted in our society are incredibly damaging and unrealistic. Who came up with the idea that you had to look or act a certain way? You should have a career, get married at a certain age—not too young or too old—and have a family. And it should be easy, or at least look that way, as though life is perfect and nothing is wrong. Raising kids is a challenge, not to mention maintaining the marriage or partnership, taking care of the house, doing laundry, making meals—and you may also have a job outside the home! Give yourself the credit you deserve, and allow yourself to see that you are unique and will do things differently from anyone else. Individually, we have our own limits; some can handle more than others and no one should be judged for that.

Do not be ashamed to ask for help; honor yourself in that way. That alone can take a huge weight off and could very well be your first challenge to overcome. It is time to remove your mask and let your true self shine.

Growing up, you are strongly shaped by the beliefs of your parents, teachers and society. As a baby, you begin as a blank slate, and all you know is love. You know nothing about imperfection or judgment; you're like a sponge, absorbing and observing everything around you. As a child, you continue discovering yourself, but this is generally when you start having to quiet your unique self, suppress your emotions and learn the socially accepted behaviors, appearances and dreams. You begin to become aware of the rewards or punishments that follow your actions. Suppressing and bottling up your feelings can result in you being weighed down and no longer knowing what to do or who you are. Each time a situation arises in which you don't express yourself, you became a little more disconnected from your true self. The further disconnected you become, the greater the hurt and pain you will feel.

Judgment of self and others, and by others, is terrible and unnecessary. If people spent more time finding the happiness within themselves, instead of focusing on others and what they are or aren't doing, we would have a much more encouraging and prosperous society. It is time to stop the cycle. Begin to build your new you, your unique and authentic you. The first and most important step is to give yourself permission to start the process to reconnect with you, which has four important steps.

***

Be Gentle on Yourself

When you are at a low point, it is hard to see anything good about yourself. By beginning the process of reading this book, you are doing an incredible thing for yourself. Celebrate this milestone of taking each step; it takes courage, strength and trust. This journey is for you and in turn will bring immense joy to you, those in your life now and all who come into your life in the future.

You will have good and bad days; there's no doubt about it. The bad days just become easier to deal with as you practice. On this journey to reconnecting with and finding you, allow yourself to be a work in progress; allow yourself to learn and discover and move forward. In hard times, it can be easy to become blocked from seeing the good, the praise, the appreciation and only see the negative. Whatever you focus on will show up in abundance. A beautiful lesson I learned early in my journey was that it was easy to put on a smile to please others, to wear a mask to fit in, but inside I felt frustrated, dishonest and fake. I came across a quote by

Maya Angelou that went perfectly with my life during that time: "If you have one smile in you, give it to the people you love. Don't be surly at home, then go out in the street and start grinning 'Good morning' at total strangers." These words made me take a step back and really reflect. I had never looked at it this way. I knew I was doing this, because my husband had mentioned it, but it never clicked until then. Once I removed the "mask," it became easier to be authentic, to just be me in all situations, inside and outside of my home. And this resulted in me being able to relax, disregard the judgments of others and, most importantly, speak my truth, which allowed me to get closer to being truly happy and reconnected with myself.

One of the most powerful tools I use for clearing negative emotion is journaling. When you feel yourself becoming frustrated or overwhelmed, take some time to be alone. This will allow you to stop the negative emotion at the top of the tornado, or as close to the top as possible. If needed, take a step back, go to a quiet space and take twenty minutes to "release journal," as I call it. For release journaling, I recommend using a piece of loose-leaf paper. The reason for this is that you are putting a lot of energy into your entries and, especially at the beginning of your healing, that energy can be quite negative. If you do your release journals in a beautiful bound journal, you will be holding on to all that negative energy, most likely stored at your bedside. That beautiful bound journal will turn into a negative symbol and a confirmation of your original feelings. Instead, I suggest you don't reread your entries, otherwise you will be reabsorbing that energy, and then immediately safely destroy the piece of paper and embrace the release.

In the heat of the moment, when you feel the intense emotions coming on, use this tool to recollect yourself, release and then continue on with what initiated the feeling. If it was a conversation or conflict with another person, explain that you need some time alone and agree to come back and resolve the issue later. If you have a partner in life, it can be helpful to have this conversation prior to a confrontation to let them know what to expect.

Celebrate Your Daily Accomplishments

Another great tool to reconnect with you is a celebration journal. You've had an amazing day, you're proud that you were happy all day, you didn't let negative emotions overcome you, you and your kids had some quality time together—whatever it may be that made you feel so great, write it down in a beautiful bound journal. Celebrate even the smallest of successes. Write those celebration moments down right after they happen, have that list going all day and reflect on it right before bed.

This is also a great tool to use when a harder moment arises in the day that you're struggling to overcome. Reflect on your celebration list and allow yourself to remember how amazing you felt in those moments.

As a busy mom, I celebrate when I've gotten some laundry done in a day and actually folded it! When I've cleaned the house and commence the countdown until the kids come back to make a mess again. I also celebrate when I've had quality time with the kids, doing something they love: made a craft or artwork, read a story, camped in our backyard. I celebrate when I've been able to have "me time" to reconnect, to scrapbook, read, meditate, do yoga. Long story short, celebrate what makes you feel happy.

Do Your Best
It's important that you're satisfying yourself and happy with what you're doing. No one else is living your life for you. You are the one who lives with the outcome of your choices. A great mentor who came in and out of my life, Thomas Bähler, author of *What You Want Wants You*, drastically changed the way I look at mistakes and failures. This shift in perspective is essential at the

beginning of your journey to reconnection. He said "mistakes" and "failures" are words that come with so much negativity and guilt. If you instead say that you made a "discovery," it changes how you feel; it's positive and progressive, and allows you to own your choices. Hearing this helped me to let go, release the negativity and give myself permission to move forward with the discoveries. Your discoveries are yours alone; they move you forward in life and build who you are and who you will become. You learn from them. If you go through life doing what pleases others, the discoveries will be a difficult process. However, if you lead with your heart and do what you feel is right in each moment, those discoveries will be an easier process as you grow, reconnect and become a stronger individual within yourself. If you feel in your heart that you are doing your best, that is all that matters.

Honor Yourself with Time for You Daily

Each day, give yourself the gift of doing something you like, something you are passionate about and love. Set aside fifteen minutes minimum every day for just you, to review your celebration journal, to meditate, to read or to just be. Abraham Hicks has some transformational guided meditations that can assist in allowing you to relax, escape and open yourself to new ideas and concepts in a gentle but effective way. If you have never meditated before, these guided meditations make it effortless. These meditations are available on YouTube and have helped me throughout my journey: "General Well-Being," "Relationship" and "Financial Well-Being."

This step is the most necessary in completing the reconnection to you. But as a mom, it can be difficult to find time for yourself that is uninterrupted. It is easy to say, "I am too busy" or "I have no time." We will get into more detail about this in Chapter 7, but do your best to catch yourself saying "I am too busy" or "I have no time," because you can always make time for the things you love, and personal growth and reconnection. This is important and you need to make it a priority. Set an intention for a certain time of the day that you will honor yourself and have you time. Some times that may work for you to commit to yourself could be first thing in the morning before the children wake up; or during their nap, if they still do; or after they have gone to bed. Become dedicated to this time to move forward and really see and feel the benefits of your accomplishments and discoveries. At the beginning of my journey, I was so excited to get up every morning, sometimes two hours before everyone else in my household, just to get that time for me to figure out exactly what I wanted and needed—to reconnect to me. I knew I was on the right track because I was motivated to continue; it felt good and freeing.

On top of the fifteen minutes you give yourself for you each day, at the end of each day, review your celebration journal. Take the time to review the good things from your day and write down at least three things that you are grateful for.

- Morning: Do something you love, meditate, read and/or just be.
- Evening: Review your celebration journal and what you're grateful for.

When you have found the right regimen that works for you, you will yearn for the time for just you each day.

***

Every day, every moment, be gentle on yourself, do your best, and honor yourself with time for. To deepen your reconnection to you, be open to doing more of what makes you happy and worry less about what others think. The more you stay true to yourself and what you want to do, and make decisions that feel good to you and are not for someone else, the closer you will become to being authentic. Remember, every mother's journey is unique and can't be compared to anyone else's; you guide your journey, choices and life. Your children are with you for a short time; enjoy them, embrace them and have fun! It can be easy to be consumed with your to-do list, but it isn't going anywhere. Relish every little moment. They are far more important than your day-to-day tasks. Especially the ones that are simply there out of fear of the judgments and expectations of others. It is time to reconnect with you, find your passion, discover your self-love and lead a happy life, without guilt or judgment. Live your life for you and what's important to you.

Tools to Reconnect with You

- Write in your release journal when you feel intense negative emotions.
- Review your celebration journal and write three things you're grateful for each day.
- Set aside fifteen minutes minimum every day for just you.

Previous Tools to Continue Using

- Do your best to read this book every day.

Chapter 2

Honor You

"It is not selfish to love yourself, take care of yourself, and to make your happiness a priority. It's necessary."
—*Mandy Hale*

Honoring yourself means giving yourself more time for you and doing things you enjoy. This will allow you to reconnect with yourself further, finding your happiness and the love within yourself again. I love the epigraph above from blogger-turned-hit-author Mandy Hale. She describes another way of thinking of taking care of yourself—it's not only for you but also for everyone who touches your life. As a mom, you build this strong foundation not only for yourself but also for your home, partner and, most importantly, children, who will make the future. If you have a strong personal foundation as a mother, you can naturally give that gift to your children. When you're happy and taking care of yourself, your partner is happy and your relationship flourishes. You're able to communicate more effectively, which creates a smoother and more open relationship. Your children see this and are happy, so your relationships with them improve and become healthier. They will learn from what they see you doing to do the same for themselves. And it doesn't stop there: these good habits will carry on to their future relationships with their own partners and kids. Giving yourself more you time will improve all the relationships in your life drastically. It is far from selfish.

Honoring you is one of the most beneficial steps on your journey of personal growth. If you have been giving yourself a minimum of fifteen minutes each day for you, to journal, read, write or do whatever makes your heart sing, you will have started to create a habit. You will also have started seeing healthy changes and adjustments in your daily life and relationships. Allow yourself the time you need to absorb this information and to process it in a way that's appropriate for you. Depending on your unique situation, you may have to reread this chapter a couple of times and do the exercises a little longer to find what works best for you. Be patient and enjoy the process.

With honoring you, comes the building of self-awareness, which according to the *Oxford English Dictionary*, is the conscious knowledge of one's own character, feelings, motives and desires. When I started my self-healing journey, the biggest transformational changes happened for me when I allowed myself to have an hour for just me every morning, before the rest of my family woke up. This time allowed me to fully connect, to dig into my health and well-being books and programs and better myself. Because I had chosen the morning for this time, it set up my day for success, as I had already put time into myself, feeding my heart and soul, and allowing me to be the best me for the day. This also made decision-making clearer for me. Find the routine that works best for you and your schedule.

Allowing yourself time every day for just you is only the beginning. The next step towards truly honoring yourself is in your day-to-day interactions with other people. When a situation arises, whether it be someone asking you for something or to do something that doesn't feel right to you, listen and pay attention to your feelings. Give yourself permission to start feeling your decisions rather than thinking about them. Your body and soul will communicate with you; you will feel whether something is right for you. It is time to start saying, "No, thank you" when something isn't right. If you can't feel what you are saying or seeking, then wait until you do. Start introducing this into your everyday life, with everyone you come in connection with and all situations that arise. Good or bad, whatever is presented, turn inward and notice how you feel. We will get deeper into discussing feeling your decisions in Chapter 4, as it is an essential part of the process of truly honoring you.

In the beginning, you may find it really hard to say no. When a difficult decision arises take the time to breathe, feel it and answer however is right for you. Don't be afraid to ask for some time to think about your answer; no answer needs to be rushed. If the other person insists they need an answer immediately, then it is not good for you and makes your decision easy. Whatever you decide, embrace it, release the guilt, and allow yourself to learn and move forward. This is all about learning—lessons and discoveries about how you feel in those moments, and the moments to follow—and becoming more in tune with yourself. Once you become more aware of your feelings, the decisions will become easier and will feel good either way. There is no guilt when you are following your heart and doing what is right for you. There may be times where you make a quick decision, and then shortly afterward think, *Why did I do that?* Just remember, everything that arises is for your own discovery and growth.

The more ways you honor yourself, the happier you become, the lighter you feel and the easier life flows. Once you become connected with what makes you happy, your perspective will change—fast. You are then more accepting of others, and all forms of judgment disappear: self-judgment, judgment of others and others' judgment of you. I love this quote by televangelist Robert

H. Schuller: "As we grow as unique persons, we learn to respect the uniqueness of others." It is so significant and accurate. The relationship you have with yourself is reflected in the relationships you have with others; this will be exemplified as you see the people around you shift and change as you grow and flourish. As you become more comfortable and confident within yourself, you will no longer feel the need to rely on other people's opinions, and you will use their suggestions as you see fit. As soon as you start valuing yourself, others will begin to as well.

Social media has been known to cause unnecessary problems and challenges for many people. Many of my clients see all these happy posts from their friends, which cause them to become more down on themselves. They feel like a failure because everyone else is happy, and they are not. The question I ask is, "Why does it make you feel worse seeing others happy?" As you progress through this book, you will find satisfaction within your own skin, regardless of what is happening with someone else. You will not feel the need to compare yourself to others. The judgment will disappear and be replaced with love for what that person is doing. There is something missing within yourself if you feel any less than or unworthy in comparison to another person. A beautiful mentor and friend of mine, holistic therapist

Leanne Oaten, really hit the nail on the head: "We each need to understand that social media is a 'profile' of our lives. A platform. A persona. The cover of a book that we only see the outside of. Posts are only a snapshot in time, and are not the moment-to-moment reality of one's life."

As you move forward in honoring yourself, some people may start disappearing from your life. You may also feel the need to separate yourself from certain relationships. During a time when you are trying to lift yourself up, it is hard to be around people who are constantly negative, as they will continue to pull you down. Two or more people together struggling with negative emotions can feed off one another, cause deeper discomfort and confirm feelings that aren't true. My suggestion is to limit your interactions with negative people to ensure your progress continues forward. In some instances this isn't possible and many of my clients have asked me, "There are a lot of negative people in my life. How can I be positive?" A key mentor of mine, motivational author Louise L. Hay, has assisted me with many of my transformation beliefs. Crucially, her wisdom has allowed me to quickly change my mindset in difficult situations and resist taking on other people's "stuff." In her book *Empowering Women*, Hay offers an amazing phrase to overcome this pitfall: "It may be true for you, but it is not true for me." So simple yet so freeing. You can say this out loud or silently to yourself when you're around someone who is saying negative things. It gives you permission to be present and assist them, but it doesn't mean you need to believe or absorb their negativity. As you start shifting your thoughts and beliefs, you will begin to notice that negative people and situations will not affect you as they once did and will even happen less frequently.

Once you are strong and confident within yourself, other people's negativity will not affect you, and you may even be able to assist them. There are some people who will naturally disappear from your life, as they can no longer relate to you, or are not getting anything from you, and are not ready to make changes in their life. Don't see this as hurtful; see it as a gift. Sometimes when the wrong people leave your life, the right things start to happen. Bring this into your awareness when looking at your friendships, family, acquaintances, companions—anyone coming into your life. Some of your relationships will grow stronger and progress to a level you never imagined possible, whereas others will fade out. This can be difficult, but trust that it is what is best for you. Know they were in your life for a reason: to allow you to learn and grow. And if they are meant to continue to be in your life, perhaps you will cross paths again in the future. Use your release journaling as necessary when you're feeling hurt, disappointment and anger. I love the analogy that many people come and go in your life; some stay for a sentence, some a paragraph, some a chapter, and some remain for the duration of the book, but each person plays a role in your story.

A new challenge is for you to introduce a weekly activity to honor you and to add to your self-care routine. This could be yoga, a fitness class, music lessons, art class, etc. Look into the activities your community offers that you enjoy. See what will fit into your and your family's schedules and budget. If you don't have an activity that you already love, try something new. Be open to new opportunities and willing to try new things. It may be just what you need at the time. As Louise L. Hay also says, "When you are willing to receive, a gift appears." If you're already attending an activity at least once a week, stay committed and enjoy it; it's your time to refresh and renew.

When I decided to add this step to my routine, I chose to try yin yoga. I had never had the opportunity to commit to a class before, but when we moved to our new home, closer to a community that offered yoga, I was in. This was one of the best decisions I have ever made. Yin yoga is an extremely slow class. It is designed to benefit the body's joints, by loosening and stretching the muscles, and stimulating and directing circulation to the connective tissues, such as the ligaments and tendons. Yin allows the body to relax and release any tension, and it provides a calm and quiet atmosphere, promoting meditation and diminishing stress. After each class, I come home refreshed and reconnected, often with some great aha moments and progressive thoughts. This is my weekly gift to myself, to honor myself and all that I do. Honoring yourself feels good; you have a craving to do it again and again because it is something you love.

The more time you dedicate to honoring yourself, the more you get to know yourself and your strengths. This process is ongoing, as there is always something to learn about yourself to deepen the connection within. You will make significant and powerful discoveries that will aid your personal growth.

As you learn and grow, so will your children. They are continuously watching and learning from you. Have you ever thought of yourself as an influencer? You may not realize it, but you have always been an influencer—you are the key influencer in your children's lives. Your children look up to you, they have so much love for you, and they will follow and imitate you. As much as you feel like you have to be strong for them, you must be strong within yourself first. When you have love and compassion for yourself, your love for them will deepen even further than you could ever imagine. When a mother heals her relationship with herself, her children have the best chance for a happy and healthy relationship with themselves. As a mom, you generally put your children and everyone else before yourself and your needs. However, if you focus on you first, it becomes easier and even more enjoyable to do things with your children and for others. All it takes is honoring yourself and taking the time to do what you enjoy daily. Once you have reconnected with yourself, you will also have empowered your kids; they will grow to be strong within themselves, and have love and compassion for themselves. As you work through this book and introduce the tools and exercises into your daily routine, keep an open mind that some of them will also be great for your children to use. This will be natural because they will see you doing them. Even if your children are adults, they will be influenced by your positive changes. It is a beautiful gift for yourself that you will in turn see in the people around you.

Just remember to be kind to yourself, fill your time with the things you love, be open and honest about your feelings, and express gratitude every day by focusing on what you are thankful for.

Tools to Honor You

- Start saying, "No, thank you."
- Make decisions slower, breathing and paying attention to how you feel and allowing yourself time to navigate those tougher situations.
  - Deal with any guilt or other negative feelings that may arise by using your release journal.
  - Introduce an activity into your schedule at least once a week.

Previous Tools to Continue Using

- Do your best to read this book every day.
- Contribute daily to your celebration journal and review it right before bed.
- Set aside fifteen minutes minimum every day just for you.

Chapter 3

Rephrase & Transform

"Nurture your mind with great thoughts, for you will never go any higher than you think."
—Benjamin Disraeli

Have you ever caught yourself saying, "I'm having a bad day," or "It's going to be one of those days," or possibly, "This is the worst day ever!"? I would like to bring something to your attention that is simple yet powerful: a bad moment does not make a day bad. It all comes down to perspective. If you continue to focus on the negative of the day, that is exactly what the day will be. Instead, if you allow yourself to have a bad moment, breathe through it and let it go, you can then refresh and focus forward on the rest of your good day. So a bad moment does not have to turn into a bad day. In fact, it will only turn into a bad day if you let it. Remember, it's a good day, with a bad moment. The bad moment is not the focus; the good day is. Ask yourself, what good has happened in your day?

By changing the way you think and what you focus on, you can change your life. Choose to focus on your positive thoughts. This will make more good things happen for you: positive attracts positive. This is where your celebration journal is really useful. In the harder moments, it can be easy to dig yourself deeper and focus on the negative, but your journal will allow you to see and relive the good of the day. Your thoughts and words are powerful and create your future. You can make a positive change for yourself today, right in this moment. Rephrasing your thoughts from negative to positive, and reframing your beliefs from limiting to empowering, is one of the most transformational tools you can use to help you on your journey. A transformational book that has assisted me on my journey is *The Four Agreements* by Don Miguel Ruiz, in which he reveals the source of limiting beliefs that rob us of joy and cause needless suffering. Based on ancient Toltec wisdom, *The Four Agreements* offers a powerful code of conduct that can rapidly transform your life into a new experience of freedom, true happiness and love.

A limiting belief is one that does not allow for change, has a definite answer and is closed-minded. For example, "I can't go out for girls' night/yoga/have me time because I have no time," or "I can't get enough sleep." Any "I can't" phrase dooms a thought before it has a chance to develop. A powerful way to allow yourself to remain open to something that you may feel isn't possible is to ask, "How *can* I?" This allows you to open your mind to possibility. For example, "How can I go out for girls' night/yoga/have me time?" Rephrasing the thought this way allows your mind to search for options instead of arriving at a definite no. Allow yourself to make a plan to make it work. What in your life can you delegate or let go to give yourself more time? Do your best in each situation; it can take time to retrain your brain to a new way of thinking.

This principle also goes for negative phrases that block you from moving forward in any part of your life: relationships, career, finances, health, etc. For instance, many of my single clients express similar thoughts when it comes to relationships: "I guess I am meant to be single," "I will never find the right partner for me and my kids," "All my relationships end in disaster." Can you see how these statements are creating exactly what they describe for the future? Instead try: "I will find my life partner at the perfect time." For my clients in a relationship, the statements are often filled with blame for their partner: "It's all their fault." Often what others do that bothers us or that we dislike is a reflection of exactly what we tend to do ourselves. Passing blame and not owning your part of the situation halts your progress forward for yourself and your relationships. Clear and open communication is needed not only with your partner but also within your own thoughts. Try: "My partner loves and respects me and my kids."

Transform your negative beliefs into empowering beliefs that will allow you to advance in your life. Be open and honest with yourself, own your mistakes, learn from them and move forward by turning them into a discovery. For this exercise, simply draw a two-column chart on a piece of paper. On one side write "Limiting Belief" and on the other write "My Empowering Belief." This is a great way for you to visualize the change and retrain your brain to create empowering beliefs instead of limiting ones. It is also a good reference for you to see and practice the empowering beliefs out loud.

Speaking the truth in all situations is freeing and feels good. Be honest about how you are truly feeling and when you know you have made a mistake. Lying will never move your progress forward and will always leave you with a weight on your shoulders and heart. Be open and honest no matter the consequence; it will make you stronger, and allow you to flourish and be the best you. This gets easier as you find your happiness and fulfill your needs. In the past, when I was not honoring myself, I would continuously give myself away. I was a people pleaser and would do anything to make others happy, even if it meant making myself miserable and giving myself away. Don't get me wrong, I love to make people happy and help when I can, but now I do it with full integrity and make sure I am honoring myself as well.

As you begin to rephrase and transform your negative thoughts, and retrain your brain to operate in a positive state, you will find that your self-worth will improve naturally, you will be able to release your guilt and your relationship with your partner will be enhanced. Reconnecting with yourself and your imagination can be difficult, but it is a pivotal step. Author Napoleon Hill created a list of physical and mental activities to allow you to do just that with ease.

Physical:

- Get enough sleep.
- Get sufficient exercise.
- Enjoy nature.
- Become comfortable with silence.
- Read a book.
- Listen to music.

Mental:

- Daydream.
- Get rid of self-limiting beliefs.
- Do not compare yourself to others.
- Suspend disbelief.
- Believe anything is possible.
- Explore unfamiliar territory
- Try new things.

- Ask yourself more questions.
- Take creative breaks.
- Brainstorm with family and friends.
- Play.
- Create.

Allow your mind to be open and aware of new opportunities that are presented to you every day. As the exercises and suggestions in this book arise, challenge yourself to give them a wholehearted try. They are all easily achievable, if you set your mind to them. Rephrasing and transforming your thoughts does not have to be difficult. It can be easy, gradual, enjoyable, empowering and enlightening. You do not need to be busy all the time; it is okay to just be. Just be in your thoughts, in silence, in your own company. Reconnecting with you and your imagination can bring incredible insights and awareness that can be beneficial to your growth and assist in transforming your thinking. It is your unique journey; progress forward in the best way for you.

Tools to Rephrase & Transform

- Turn "I can't" statements into "How can I?"
- Exchange negative thoughts for positive thoughts.
- Change limiting beliefs to empowering beliefs.
- Reconnect with you and your imagination.

Previous Tools to Continue Using

- Do your best to read this book every day.
- Contribute daily to your celebration journal and review it right before bed.
- Set aside fifteen minutes minimum every day just for you.
- Start making decisions by feeling instead of thinking.

Chapter 4

Overcome Self-Doubt

"Believe in yourself and all that you are. Know that there is something inside you that is greater than an obstacle."
—*Christian D. Larson, thought leader, author and teacher*

It's easy to feel self-doubt in a world filled with critics, but who is a worse critic than yourself? Often I see my clients try to prove their worth by doing what makes other people happy. They believe they aren't good enough unless others are telling them they are. I also used to live this way. I always leaned on others to reassure me that what I was doing was okay, but I would never ask their opinion for fear of disapproval and disappointment. When criticisms came, I would succumb to self-doubt, telling myself I would never succeed and I was a big failure, undeserving of anything good in my life. I had no confidence to believe in myself. I tried to do what would satisfy others and make them proud. When I went to college to become a natural health practitioner, I endured a lot of criticism from my loved ones, as this was not a field they understood or could relate to; in their eyes, it was not credible. Even before I received my diploma, I had already decided that I would become an electrician. Instead of pursuing my dream, I followed a career that I knew everyone around me would accept and approve. I received praise from all my loved ones and even complete strangers, which persuaded me to keep going.

Living off the praise of others and doing what makes them happy has detrimental effects. I was dishonoring myself with my career. I was on the wrong path. I was miserable, angry, frustrated, lashing out, and worst of all, I wasn't present with my family. I was just plodding through life until my husband finally got through to me, with his sorrowful expressions, words of pain and sympathetic emotions. He opened my eyes to see that I was hurting not only myself but also him and our children. I had to hit rock bottom, the bottom of my tornado, before realizing I had to do what would make me happy. That was when I found my way to pull myself out of my self-destructive tornado and deep depression, onto my journey of self-healing to better myself.

My change in direction from natural healing to electrician was a decision made for other people, but my return to natural healing was one I made with my heart. I knew it was what I needed to do; however, I was scared and unsure whether I could do it. I was full of self-doubt. I would get up at five every morning to dig into my healing journey: reading, journaling and doing online courses. I was truly dedicated to finding myself. After about six months of really digging in, I felt truly passionate and believed in what I was doing. I was confident and ready to go to the people closest to me, who had rejected me in the past, and test my strength. I shared my story and explained why I was changing my path. To my surprise, they supported me.

Fear is an unpleasant emotion caused by the belief that someone or something is dangerous, and likely to cause pain or a threat. Now I look at fear completely differently. What is the worst that could happen? Other people don't agree? They say no way? Those sentiments couldn't hurt me, unless I believed them. My own self-doubt was holding me back the whole time; it had nothing to do with anyone else. Opinions are just another person's way of looking at you. Be open to different opinions, but recognize that "truth" is not real unless you believe it. These opinions brought forward by others can allow you to understand yourself better and deepen your self-awareness.

The more time you dedicate to yourself and your journey, the deeper you will connect with yourself, your passions, your purpose and what you want, with ease and at a faster rate. This will result in a happier you, quicker. Throughout your journey, you will recon with yourself, find or rediscover the hobbies and activities you really like to do and, most importantly, regain the love for yourself again, your self-love. That will bring increased self-esteem and confidence. They all go hand-in-hand: self-love = self-esteem + confidence. As your self-love grows, your self-doubt with decrease. The clearer you are on your intent, the more you are self-assured and confident, resulting in the extinguishment of self-doubt.

The truer you are to yourself in the decisions you make, and all aspects of your life, the more self-confidence you will have. When faced with the need to make a decision, notice how you feel. Are you feeling at ease? Tense? Scared? Angry? Happy? Excited? There are many emotions that come with making a decision. If you notice them, it will make the process a lot easier. I feel decisions in my heart and chest area. The more I practiced feeling rather than thinking about my decisions, the easier they were to make. If you really do not want to do something, but you say yes anyway, the energy you put in will not be pleasant or healthy. But this technique makes it so that those situations aren't a problem anymore. You're able to say no without difficulty when the decision isn't right for you. It's time to start saying, "No, thank you." If you're able to release the worry of other people judging you or of hurting their feelings, and make wholehearted decisions according to what is best for you, you will see drastic changes in how you feel.

Another struggle that I had, as well as many of my clients, is apologizing. Do you have a hard time apologizing, or ever find yourself apologizing when it's really not necessary, or possibly both? Apologizing used to be my nemesis. I used to throw "sorry" out there for the most minimal things. Because of a lack of self-confidence and immense self-doubt, I pretty much apologized for walking the earth. For example, if someone cut me off while I was walking down the street, I would say sorry. If someone bumped or ran into me, I would say sorry. However, when an apology was truly needed, I believed it was the hardest thing to do, yet didn't understand why I felt this way. In those moments, I can remember thinking, *Just say sorry and make this situation better. If you would just say sorry, you could really improve this situation. Why can't you say sorry?!* When I couldn't apologize right away, I would then dig myself into a deeper mess by convincing myself that I had waited too long now to apologize and it was too late.

This is another situation where stopping yourself at the top of the tornado can be beneficial. At my very first meeting with my counselor I was able to look at apologizing in a whole new light. I am so grateful to her for this simple gift. She told me that I needed to adopt the perspective: "I am not apologizing for who I am or how I feel; I am apologizing for a behavior I had that I didn't like." She also shared with me that feeling anger doesn't make you a bad person, but rather indicates our body needs attention, compassion and healing. Ever since she imparted this amazing view to me, I have had no problem apologizing when needed.

This is a release in itself and allows for difficult situations to be resolved and rectified so that you can move forward. In the beginning, you might start taking care of yourself for others, but quickly, you will enjoy how you're feeling and start doing it for you. I started my journey for my husband and kids, but almost instantly, I was feeling the rewards for myself, which reflected in all my relationships. This process is all about finding yourself again, so you can be the best you— for everyone in your life, now and in the future.

These first steps, to reconnect with you, honor you, rephrase and transform the way you think, and overcome self-doubt, can be the hardest. Be as gentle as you can on yourself. Change is possible. Dedication to yourself is key and will be needed to push through the difficult situations that arise. Just remember: they are only there to make you stronger. You will become what you expect of yourself, so believe you are what you desire to be.

Using cue cards, symbol cards, vision cards or sticky notes around your home can act as a powerful reminder tool of what is important to you and retrain your brain to keep yourself going forward. These cards can have beautiful uplifting phrases, pictures, goals, reminders to breathe or smile; they can have anything on them that will lift you up and brighten your day. Personalize them and have fun. Place these cards where you will see them frequently; the bathroom mirror is a great place, as you will see them every day when you first wake up, throughout the day and right before you go to bed. Repetition is powerful. Here are a few examples to get you started:

- "I am in the process of reconnecting with me."
- "Take three deep breaths."
- "I am in the process of loving me again."
- "I will do what makes me happy today."

As you grow and progress forward, these cue cards will change. It is time to change your cards when maybe the message is not quite right, so you're resisting it, you have lost enthusiasm, it starts looking old or dirty or your vision has changed. Enjoy this process; it can be really fun to see what is presented to you once you are clear and put intentions and visions out there.

The importance of this chapter is to help guide your journey on a path and timeline that *feels* right to you, that is not led by someone else and their satisfaction. If you do not stay true to you, your journey will bring you right back to the beginning to try again. Just as mine did after my third child was born and I was hit with a deep depression. At first, I didn't listen; I brushed it off, but it came back with a vengeance a couple of years later, after my fourth child was born. Then I listened with due attention. But only when it *feels* right in your heart, when you are ready, when your decisions feel good and are made with ease, will you know what is right for you. Only you have the answers for you, so trust yourself. "Mistakes" happen, but mistakes are really discoveries. Allow yourself to learn and grow from them; they will make you stronger if you let them.

At the beginning of any change, self-doubt will arise. It will be most prominent in the early stages, while you're gaining confidence, but eventually it won't affect you as it once did. Once you know from within that you are good enough, doubt and other people's opinions won't alter your path or decisions. A great exercise to get a lot of your doubts out of the way is to make a list of them, see them and acknowledge the questions that arise. Determine what obstacles they bring and design a strategy to overcome them. An easy way to do this is to draw a chart with three columns: Doubt, Obstacle and Strategy. An example of a common obstacle is not having enough money. Acknowledge it, see what questions come up and make a strategy to get enough money. For example, the doubt is "I can't do it," the obstacle is "I don't have enough money," and then a strategy would be to get a part-time job that works with your schedule, or sell a few things that no longer serve you.

The limiting belief to empowering belief exercise can assist with this as well. Sometimes a strategy is overcoming a limiting belief. For example, the limiting belief "I will never be happy" can be redirected into the empowering belief "I deserve to be happy." When self-doubt sets in, it is easy to fall back into old patterns of keeping busy and forgetting about what you truly love and want. This is why this exercise is so important.

Mindset is an incredibly powerful tool. When your mind is not in the right place and you are doubting yourself, you are continuing to support that destructive mindset; you are limiting and hurting yourself. When you believe you are not good enough, you are only confirming that for yourself. Even if when you were growing up, someone told you that you would never succeed at doing what you love, it is only confirmed if *you* believe it. Nothing anyone else says to you is true unless *you* believe it. Retrain your mind to be self-confident with the exercises in this chapter and review them daily. You can do anything you want, if you believe in yourself. Like the tornado, when self-doubt or limiting beliefs arise, stop them at the top of the spiral, acknowledge what they bring and redirect them towards what you desire: your empowering belief.

By rephrasing and transforming the way you phrase things, you can retrain your brain to change self-doubt into self-confidence and assurance. You can go from limiting to empowering, and from absolutely not to anything is possible. You are in control of what happens in your life, so allow yourself to progress forward with ease and grace, because when you believe in yourself, anything can happen. Believing in yourself is an imperative part of the journey to find the happiness and love within you. This will be unique to you and will take time, but gradually it will become attainable, and as a result you will be able to quickly overcome self-doubt and life's trials. Take your time with this step, as it is very personal.

Tools to Overcome Self-Doubt

- Feel decisions instead of thinking.
- Make cue cards with inspirational quotes to brighten your day.
- Use the Doubt/Obstacle/Strategy exercise when self-doubt arises.
- Use the Limiting Belief vs. Empowering Belief exercise to assist.

Previous Tools to Continue Using

- Do your best to read this book every day.
- Contribute daily to your celebration journal and review it right before bed.
- Set aside fifteen minutes minimum every day just for you.
- Start making decisions by feeling instead of thinking.
- Turn "I can't" statements into "How can I?"
- Exchange negative thoughts for positive thoughts.

Chapter 5

Reflect & Resolve

"If you are always trying to be normal, you will never know how amazing you can be."
—*Maya Angelou*

Traveling through a journey like this, through the thick and thin of past emotions that were stored and never dealt with, that can go as far back as your early childhood, can result in a volcanic eruption. Volcanoes are a manifestation of blazing power that is stored deep in the earth. When the magma and gas build up, the volcano will erupt and can explode, emitting lava, rock and ash into the air. Similarly, if you bottle up all your emotions, one day, you will explode.

Many of my clients experience a very similar scenario. In the past, when I was giving myself away without honoring myself every day, I would become easily frustrated and irritated. I was not great at dealing with conflict, and I was afraid to hurt someone's feelings, even if they had hurt mine. I would neglect the feelings. If someone, for example, did something that upset me or made me angry, instead of talking about it, I would ignore it. I would hold it within myself, until one day, BOOM, I would explode like a volcano for the smallest and most insignificant reason at the people I loved most: my children and husband. Here is another opportunity to live your life with integrity and deal with situations that you feel you should confront or resolve as they arise. It may not be easy, but it is important not to leave anything unfinished and holding you back, so that you can live your life to the fullest extent, with less stress, frustration, anxiety and unnecessary lashing out. The following are three key components to preventing a volcano:

- As situations arise that do not sit well with you, deal with them right away and resolve them.
- Do not neglect your feelings for the benefit of someone else who may be hurting you; speak your truth.
- Share this practice with your children, so that they know it is okay to talk openly about their feelings if something is upsetting them.

Acknowledge the emotions as they arise and work to release them immediately, so that you can progress forward without the extra weight of an unresolved situation. Often there can be pain from the past that was caused by someone else: a past relationship, family member or friend. When left unresolved, this can result in you coming up against a brick wall as you try to progress forward; the very thing that is holding you back. Keep in mind that this situation does not own you and it does not determine your future—you do. Depending on how deep the pain is and your individual situation, you may have to do the following exercise a number of times. You will know when it is released, as it will no longer affect you.

Use release journaling from Chapter 1 to assist you. As an extension of that exercise, give yourself twelve minutes to just write it out. Have a glass of water by your side, set a gentle timer, that has a soft alarm and won't startle you, so that you don't have to worry about the time and can truly focus on the task. Use a blank loose-leaf piece of paper, and while you write, do not think, or worry about punctuation or spelling—just write. You might be surprised by what comes up. Often it is things you think you have let go but haven't been completely released. Or it might show you what you need to do next. This will be an individual experience, but it is essential for the rest of your journey. Allow any emotion that arises to flow freely, breathe deeply and do not stop until the timer rings. Please do this exercise now, prior to completing this chapter.

Did anything come up for you that was surprising? Maybe it was something you felt you had already dealt with, but it came up anyway. Something may have come up that needs further attention to allow you to move forward. If this is the case, continue to do this exercise daily for twelve days, twelve minutes a day. This may take some time, depending on the depth of the pain, but remember: it does not own you. What is in the past has brought you to where you are today, but it does not dictate your future—you do.

Occasionally, deep darkness from the past can have devastating effects on our present. This could be mentally, physically, emotionally, spiritually, possibly all of the above, or a combination. At times, it is imperative to seek assistance from a professional counselor or psychologist, to work through the effects of something from the past. There is no shame in doing so. Professionals are there for a reason and should be used when necessary. It is safe and always confidential. Allow yourself to take the steps needed to release what is not serving you.

As you reflect and resolve past stored emotions and situations, you will begin to find that it becomes easier to continue forward on your journey of self-healing. You will no longer allow unsettled situations to be prolonged but will handle them right away. This release of bottled-up emotions will allow you to become more relaxed when unexpected situations arise that were not what you had visualized or planned initially, which may cause disappointment, frustration or anger. These situations come occasionally as a part of life—almost daily when you're a mom. When this happens, take a breath, slow down and allow yourself to shift your emotion from reaction to choice. Especially with your children, if they aren't getting their way, or frantically interrupt something you're doing, or start fighting, yelling and screaming; for example, slow down your reaction, take some time to reflect and understand their perspective, release the accompanying emotions, and then respond. Reflect, Release, and then Resolve. Just like you, your children need to learn the skills to release their overwhelming and overpowering emotions. Without guidance they will learn to bottle it up and begin to build their explosive volcano.

One thing I noticed right away when I started using this tool was that my kids naturally responded better and more calmly. For example, when they didn't get the response they were hoping for and started freaking out, I would just breathe, let them get it all out—sometimes privately in their room—and once they calmed down, we would talk about it. This was much

more effective than me just yelling at them to go to their
room and leaving it unresolved, which would just
intensify their emotions. Now, they process emotions
much quicker, by slowing down their reaction, thinking
about it, and then talking about it.

Another example that was so powerful and
confirming for me was the response between my
children. My youngest daughter just loved bugging her
older brother by stealing his toys to see if she could get a
reaction. He would respond with a frenzy of yelling,
screaming and crying, asking for them back. She loved it
and wouldn't give them back. Now, after some guidance
and coaching, he calmly asks for them back and makes a
deal for a toy she can have so that they can play together.
My daughter responds by doing exactly what he asks!
This confirms that the energy you give out is the energy
you will get back. It takes some extra time at first for
your children to learn and for you to teach, but soon,
they can release their own emotions and resolve conflicts
in a calm and effective way.

In life, unfortunately, there are unforeseen
circumstances that can change plans in a moment. The
power of emotion is such that it can change in an instant,
from excitement and happiness to anger and frustration.
Before I reconnected with myself, if I visualized or
expected a situation to happen in a particular way and it

didn't turn out, I would let it ruin my entire day, and take it out on the people around me. I would be angry and frustrated at everything and everyone. Once I began my self-healing, honored myself daily and started doing things that I loved, I became more relaxed and open to the unexpected. I do my best not to have expectations, to just let life happen and enjoy it. This brings more joy, humor and playfulness in the trying times. When I noticed this change in myself, I also noticed the change in my children. They could handle unexpected situations better as well. Now, if they become upset or disappointed, we can have a conversation and shift the emotions. Emotions can change in an instant. Life is far too short to sweat the small stuff.

When you notice an old response has changed, celebrate it! Embrace the moments when you are proud of yourself and fill your whole being with that empowerment. Remember to write, in depth, how you're feeling in your celebration journal, so that when a circumstance arises in which you need a boost, you can revisit how amazing you felt. This exercise will empower you during times of disappointment. You will find when you feel confident and proud of what you do, and there is no self-doubt, others will feel your energy is strong, confident and empowered, and generally they will support you.

I found when I became more confident and my self-worth increased, I was more certain and self-assured about the decisions I made. I had no problem expressing my dreams to people who in the past would have kiboshed them. I believe this is because of the confident energy I emitted. Energy is a powerful influence. We are all made up of energy, emit energy and feel energy. Emotions are energy. For example, if you are feeling strong, confident and empowered, you will project that energy. Have you ever noticed your energy being lifted by someone just by being close to them? Receiving a hug, or a smile? When someone is emitting a strong positive energy, they uplift those around them. The opposite is also true. Have you ever been around someone and they just give you an unsure feeling, or the heebie-jeebies? This is energy too. If you were to zoom in on your DNA and look at an atom, you could see the little movements of energy.

A great visual for energy is Kirlian photography, which is a collection of photographic techniques used to capture the phenomenon of electrical coronal discharges. Kirlian images demonstrate the energy throughout living things. They show how the energy of one living thing can have a strong influence over another living thing. Thoughts and feelings affect everything around us; what we are feeling is mirrored in the world around us.

Sometimes when the actions of another affect you, self-reflection is needed. Often, when there is something about another that you do not like, something they have done, or something they regularly do, it can be a true reflection of yourself. Ask yourself, "Do I do those things?"

A powerful tool that you can use to help you with this is the mirroring exercise, which allows you to discover more about yourself, and learn and grow without judgment.

Create a list of five to ten things that annoy you about the people around you. For example:

- My husband doesn't listen; he is not present with me.
- People are competitive and always trying to prove they are better than you.
- My family is so negative.
- I am surrounded by dream crushers
- People talk behind your back.

Now create a list of five to ten things you enjoy, appreciate and love about the people around you. For example:

- I have a lot of supportive friends.

- There are so many loving people.

- People are becoming open and interested.

- I can feel comfortable about my dreams.

Reflect on your second list, and feel gratitude and appreciation for the individuals who have shown you these things. Consider how you can get to know who you are through your relationships and experiences with other people. Reflecting on the first list can bring forward awareness of things you are unconsciously doing that you do not appreciate being done to you by others. Also, the opposite: people will do great things for you, usually because you have done the same for them. The energy you are putting out is what you will attract. You have a huge impact on what is happening around you, both negative and positive. Notice your surroundings, and then notice how you are feeling and what you have been doing. Do not blame others, but identify tendencies within yourself, release the old patterns and rectify them from there. Create what you want to see in your life by being your own mirror. Celebrate these moments of new awareness as they occur.

Allow yourself to reflect on situations that arise from the past and resolve them right away to continue forward weightlessly and with ease. If you truly believe in yourself and you have a dream, you can make it happen. It's time to let go of what's holding you back.

Tools to Reflect & Resolve

- Reflect on past emotions and what has been holding you back.
- Write in your release journal for twelve minutes a day for twelve days. Remember to breathe and allow yourself to experience whatever emotions arise. Do not suppress them, so that you can achieve a full release.
- Reflect, Release and Resolve
  - This can also be a great exercise for your children
- Mirror exercise

Previous Tools to Continue Using

- Do your best to read this book every day.
- Contribute daily to your celebration journal and review it right before bed.
- Set aside fifteen minutes minimum every day just for you.

- Feel your decisions.
- Turn "I can't" statements into "How can I?"
- Exchange negative thoughts for positive thoughts.
- Once a week, reflect on your motivational cue cards; replace as needed.
- Doubt/Obstacle/Strategy exercise
- Limiting Belief vs. Empowering Belief exercise

Chapter 6

Find Your Passions

*"Finding your passion isn't just about careers and money.
It's about finding your authentic self. The one you've
buried beneath other people's needs."*
—*Kristin Hannah, bestselling author of* The Nightingale

Now that you're becoming more aware of your feelings
and how different situations affect you, it's time to find
your passions, the things you love to do, that deepen
your self-love. Before you started reading this book, you
weren't doing enough of the things that you love to
satisfy yourself and be truly happy. Maybe you thought
you were, but you may now be aware that you have not.
When you're living a life of passion, doing what makes
you happy and what you love, your soul is singing. You're
truly happy, your chest feels open, light, and you feel at
ease. You're protected from those deep, dark depressive
feelings, because when you're whole and living your
passion, you are strong, in love with you, and it is
impossible to fall too deep. You are able to stop yourself
at the top of the tornado, redirect discoveries and use
them to move forward. It is easier to recover from those
harder moments of self-doubt.

What is it that you love to do? What makes your
heart sing and that you can't get enough of? If you're
unsure of what you love to do, you're not alone. Many
people feel the same. I believe this is directly related to
the increased rates of stress, anxiety and depression in
our society. Research published in 2006 in the *American
Journal of Psychiatry* found that major depression rates
for American adults increased from 3.33 percent to 7.06
percent from 1991 through 2002. Depression is
considered a worldwide epidemic, with 5 percent of the
global population suffering from the condition, according
to the World Health Organization.

Feeling unhappy and not having a passion, hobby
or activity we love can lead us to feeling the need to keep
busy—distracted. Some feel if they are busy, it makes
them look successful. I once read an inspiring blog called
Are You Addicted to Busyness? that opened my eyes to a
whole new outlook. The key points that came out of this
blog for me were the idea of busyness as a badge of
honor that makes some people feel important, valuable
and worthy. As a society, we do not know how to be
bored. Often, we are looking for some sort of stimulant.
Part of this is because of not knowing how to deal with
our emotions and how to be alone. Take a moment and
reflect on your daily activities: Are you busy and always
doing something throughout the entire day? Are you able

to just be, or do you need to always be doing something? Do you find when you are taking time for you that your mind tends to wander? Here is another idea to ponder: being busy is armor against vulnerability, a numbing strategy. An amazing quote by scholar, author and public speaker Brené Brown sums it up: "We are a culture of people who have bought into the idea that if we stay busy enough, the truth of our lives won't catch up to us."

A powerful exercise that may assist you with extending your "you time" is Just Be. Find a quiet space and allow yourself ten minutes to just be with you. This means no phone, no books, nothing, just you sitting there, feeling and seeing what your response is. Having downtime forces you to notice what is coming up. You may find this really difficult. You may feel like you should be doing something, and you may not last the ten minutes. In these moments, it is easy to become distracted by your to-do list, but know that nothing must be done today. Or these ten minutes of you time might feel amazing, and you might want more. This exercise can tell you a lot about yourself. Whatever your response, enjoy the process and the time. You deserve it and it will most definitely benefit you.

Make a list of how you feel and what comes up when you're just sitting in silence. When I first did this exercise, my list was:

- I feel like I am neglecting my husband.
- I am uncomfortable with boredom.
- I have a tendency to feel unworthy and unlovable unless I'm overachieving.
- I feel like my house should always be clean and the chores always done.

The second step to this exercise is Making Peace with Inaction. Ask yourself: How does being inactive or bored make me feel? My list the first time I did this exercise was:

- I feel guilty taking time for myself. I only feel comfortable when no one is around and no one is aware.
- My kids must be in bed so that I'm not putting my needs ahead of anyone else's.

To find your passions, eliminate unhappiness and any addiction to busyness; take the time you need for you. It is critical to take care of yourself and satisfy your needs before assisting others. As a mom, that comes with the job description. This is why it is so important to take care of you first, so that you can be the best mother for your children and enjoy your time with them, instead of being stressed out because you're hiding behind your to-do list and not feeding your soul.

Allow your children to assist you with your to-do list. You do not need to do everything yourself. Delegate. Children really do love to help. Some ideas follow for age-appropriate chores for kids, depending on your child's individual abilities.

Age 2–3:
- Pick up/put away toys.
- Unload the dishwasher (silverware, plastic cups, Tupperware).
- Collect dirty clothes.
- Put clothes in the dirty clothes hamper.

Age 4–5:
- Load the dishwasher.
- Set the table.
- Clear the table.
- Feed pets.

Age 6–8:
- Help with meal prep (wash produce, find ingredients, simple cutting).
- Clean bathroom sinks, counters, toilets.
- Put laundry away.

- Sweep.
- Vacuum.
- Collect mail.
- Fold/hang laundry.

Age 9–11

- Make simple meals.
- Take out garbage/recycling.
- Wash/dry clothes.
- Mop floors.

Age 12–14

- Clean tub/shower.
- Make full meals.
- Clean out fridge/freezer.
- Mow yard.
- Supervise younger children's chores.

Allow your kids to help you; it doesn't do anyone any favors for you to do it all. This is a challenge for you to let go of your way of doing things. The chores may not be done perfectly or how you would do them, but it helps and is less for you to do. And the children are left feeling accomplished and proud. This also teaches them necessary life skills. I have met quite a few people who move out of their parents' home but have never cleaned a bathroom, cooked a meal or done their own laundry.

The more they do it, the better they will get, but if you don't let them try, then how will they learn?

In my family, my kids know we are a team; we work together to do the chores. They are not one person's job; they are all of our responsibility. Plus, the more they contribute, they more they honor and respect the house and its cleanliness. A really great tool to make this process easy is called Easy Daysies® Magnetic Schedules For Kids. This system was created by a mom/teacher, is made with 70 percent recycled materials, and helps children feel safe and confident knowing what is happening next in their day. It has won eleven awards and helps kids as young as preschoolers become more cooperative, confident and independent by showing them the "shape of the day." You can use it for a single activity, like bedtime, going potty or after-school routine, or to plan the whole day. This system makes for easy and stress-free mornings. It is wonderful for helping kids of any age, and children with special needs, deal with event transition, executive functioning and anxiety. Easy Daysies is recommended by name by child psychologists, occupational therapists, and speech and language pathologists. My kids love it; they are so proud to remove the magnets as they accomplish each task!

As a child, can you remember ever saying, "I'm bored" and seeking out an adult to give you an idea of what to do? Being "bored" is actually a really amazing opportunity that allows you to connect with yourself and learn how to be with just you, to enjoy the time with yourself. I believe this is a really important lesson that we also need to allow our children to experience. There are far too many circumstances when children are running from one activity to the next, or have some form of entertainment or stimulant at all times. Spending time alone is not a bad thing. In fact, it is a necessity and should be an important part of our daily routine.

Once you become comfortable with the Just Be exercise, you can combine this ten minutes of you time with the fifteen minutes you have already been implementing from Chapter 1, allowing at least twenty-five minutes per day just for you. This will allow you to connect even deeper within to discover the things you truly love to do, which will lead to your passions and dreams. This will give you an amazing drive that opens your heart, allowing for more opportunity and giving you purpose.

If you already know what your passion is, incorporate it as much as possible into this time each day. However, if you're struggling to find things that you love to do, start exploring new activities and hobbies. Here are some examples of passions that may assist you on your journey to find yours:

- Hobbies at home: cooking, baking, knitting
- Sports
- Enriched hobbies: educational pursuits that improve the mind, e.g., learning a new language, music lessons, blogging
- Social activities: volunteering, game nights, clubs
- Creative hobbies: art, scrapbooking, drawing, writing, dancing, painting
- Collecting: antiques, art

Do any of these spike your interest? Take note and see what you can find in your community. Sometimes when you're not sure where to start, simply start saying yes. When family or friends invite you to something you'd normally say no to, say yes instead. During this process, you will learn a lot about yourself, you will begin to enjoy your own company, and you will find an amazing shift will happen with all your relationships as well. As you connect more with yourself, you will connect more with the people around you, allowing for increased presence and further understanding. Maybe there have been barriers up, insecurities or lack of confidence present that have stopped you from doing more of what you love. You have already eliminated a lot of your barriers in previous chapters. With the earlier exercises in overcoming self-doubt and letting go of what is holding you back (guilt, other people's opinions), you should be feeling a lot more free to be yourself. Bear in mind that it may be necessary to revisit past chapters as you progress forward in your journey.

The exercises in this chapter can be extremely beneficial for your children. I highly recommend getting your kids involved and sharing these exercises with them. Imagine if you were able to have all these tools from this book so far as a child and be so comfortable with the idea of honoring yourself, doing what you love, focusing inward rather than outward, throughout your entire life? You would be an entirely different person. In fact, you wouldn't need a lot of the tools presented. The best part is that it's never too late to start! By implementing these practices into your life, and your children's lives, you are already making an amazing change for the future. Your children are so fortunate to have you. Introducing these exercises into your children's routines will allow them to connect with the things that they really love, instead of perhaps following what their friends are doing. These exercises will allow your children to connect within them to what makes them happy. This in turn will feed their souls, giving them confidence to make smarter choices for themselves, and living an all around advantageous life. Finally, you and your children will be able to connect on a different level as well.

Tools to Find Your Passions:

- Ask yourself, "Am I addicted to busyness?"
    - Take ten minutes a day for just you.
    - Just Be exercise
    - Making Peace with Inaction exercise
- Delegate some chores to kids.
- Write a passion list.
    - Start saying yes.
- Invite your children to do these exercises also.

Previous Tools to Continue Using

- Do your best to read this book every day.
- Contribute daily to your celebration journal and review it right before bed.
- Set aside fifteen minutes minimum every day just for you.
- Feel your decisions.
- Turn "I can't" statements into "How can I?"

- Exchange negative thoughts for positive thoughts.
- Once a week, reflect on your motivational cue cards; replace as needed
- Doubt/Obstacle/Strategy exercise
- Limiting Belief vs. Empowering Belief exercise
- Keep saying, "No, thank you."
- Write in your release journal for twelve minutes a day for twelve days.
- Reflect, Release and Resolve
- Mirror exercise

Chapter 7

Discover Self-Love

"We must be our own before we can be another's."
—*Ralph Waldo Emerson*

The more you are feeling connected with yourself, the more you will love yourself. You will be excited, motivated and driven to continue on this path to fully connecting with yourself, your purpose and your self-love. The *Oxford English Dictionary* defines self-love as the "regard for one's own well-being and happiness (chiefly considered as a desirable rather than narcissistic characteristic)." Loving yourself is not conceited. Self-love is acceptance, kindness, encouragement and caring. A conceited person has excessive pride, thinks they're better than others and is determined to prove it in thoughts and words. When you have love for yourself, doubts disappear, fears fade and a comfort develops that even when you're alone becomes a place of solace. Keep your energy and excitement up; keep doing the things that you love, or exploring to find "your thing." Continue to be open to new things; you never know, you may find a new, fun hobby that you really enjoy. This will drive you forward in your journey to find complete love for yourself.

At the beginning of my journey, and most of my clients', there were a lot of self-consciousness and self-confidence issues. With the release of judgment from yourself and others, it becomes easier to just be and begin to love every bit of yourself. I cannot express the importance of this piece; it is key to the foundational work that will set you up to be able to maintain your happiness and self-love for life.

A common self-consciousness issue after having children is body image. After I had children, I decided I should not wear a bikini anymore because of the way I thought my body looked. I had really low self-esteem. It wasn't until about eight months into my self-healing journey that I felt confident enough to disregard the opinions of others. It never really matters what another person thinks; it starts from within you, your beliefs, and your self-love. I had gotten to the point where I was the only one who needed to be satisfied with how my body looked—that was the transformational moment. I had completely released the fear of judgments from others. After I went out for the first time in a bikini in public, I was relieved and proud. I couldn't believe I hadn't done that sooner!

None of our bodies can be compared to anyone else's; we are all unique and beautiful. Do what you want and what makes you feel comfortable. Don't let the thought of what other people might be thinking hold you back. If you want to wear a bikini, wear a bikini! Most of the time "other people" are too busy worrying about how they look to worry about you. If they do think about you, it's because they have insecurities of their own. Once you're able to give yourself the gift of releasing self-judgment and the worry of judgment coming from others, you will feel so free and your self-esteem with improve drastically. Self-esteem goes hand-in-hand with self-love. As one grows, so does the other.

A powerful exercise, that I highly recommend you start doing every day, and that will vastly improve your self-love is a second Mirror exercise. Look into your eyes in the mirror and tell yourself that you love you. Tell yourself the things you love about yourself. The list may be small at first, but as you grow, so will your list. Do your best to maintain eye contact with yourself. This may be difficult at first. Again, be patient; it will get easier. Do this every day, a couple times a day, whenever you are in the bathroom. Tell yourself at least one thing you love about yourself looking into your eyes in the mirror.

During this process you are going to discover so much about yourself that you never realized before. By self-reflecting, and learning through books and life discoveries, you are uncovering the unique you, developing a deeper self-love with each day, with respect and understanding. The more comfortable you become with yourself the more authentic you will be, and the easier it will be to make decisions that are right for you. When you are true to yourself and have found your self-love, the quality and integrity of your life improves too. They are equal and grow together. Self-esteem = self-love = quality and integrity of life. Only when you are being entirely true to yourself, will you be able to be completely honest and true with others as well, resulting in a life of integrity.

Integrity is one of the most valuable traits you can have. Integrity is the quality of being honest and having strong moral principles—moral uprightness. It is also the state of being whole and undivided. Can you see how this is vitally important? Not only is it important to have integrity moving forward but also cleaning up what is unfinished from your past and present. An exercise that may assist you with this is to look at all aspects of your life—personal, professional, financial, health and well-being, relationships—and face what is unfinished. Use a page for each heading with two columns; in one column make a list of what is unfinished, and in the other write how you will complete them.

A common example of something unfinished in a relationship is planning to have a weekly date night, but it never happens. To complete this, sit down together, compare schedules and marked them on the calendar each month, and then find time for date night. Allotting this time for each other can vastly improve your relationship and open the opportunity for conversations you may not be able to have regularly. For unfinished finances, if there is a debt that you want to pay off, make a step-by-step plan to do so; for example, each month a certain amount of money automatically goes to that debt. This exercise can take a lot of weight off your shoulders and allow you to begin the process of releasing what might be holding you back.

Whatever has gotten you excited, lit up and motivated to take the time for you each day, which we learned about in Chapter 2, whether you have found a new hobby you enjoy, you are planning to change your profession or you are simply feeling better about who you are, share your passion and experiences with your family and friends. I was so driven to share my personal discoveries and passions with anyone who would listen, which allowed them to become more real and improved my self-love and confidence. Often after sharing my experience with someone, an enthusiasm would emerge in that person. The more you share your journey with others, the more you will feel it, the more it will become reality and the more support you will receive. It is incredible how your energy will feed others, and they will be more apt to understand and support you. When you understand your life's meaning and purpose, you will become more alive and aligned with who you are, increasing your self-love.

Be the author of your own life, creating space to embrace learning. Allow yourself to have discoveries through mistakes, life lessons and experiences. If you remain open and allow yourself to just be on a daily basis, you will strengthen your self-love, and continue to grow and prosper. As your own relationship with yourself improves, so will all the relationships in your life. This is because you are relying on you for love, instead of looking for it in someone else. I'm reminded of a powerful quote from *The Mastery of Love* by Don Miguel Ruiz: "If you take your happiness and put it in someone's hands, sooner or later, she is going to break it. If you give your happiness to someone else, she can always take it away. Then if happiness can only come from inside of you and is the result of your love, you are responsible for your happiness." This book vastly improved the way I viewed relationships. As your relationship with yourself improves, it becomes easier to let your heart guide you to where you need to go and

what you need to do. Be open to the signs and
opportunities that will begin to arise on your journey.
This will lead you to what's next for you. Things will
begin to line up and become clear as you become more
connected with yourself, your path and your self-love. To
this day, I love receiving small confirmations that I am
going in the right direction.

One of my favorite sequences of confirmations
began when I was seeing my counselor and I had
determined that I wanted to go back to my roots as a
natural health practitioner. I wanted to assist people on
their own journeys of self-discovery. I started looking for
an office space that I could practice out of and replied to
a few ads online. At my next meeting with my counselor,
she started talking about my office space. I was baffled; I
didn't understand how she knew I was looking and that I
was going to tell her all about it at that appointment! She
informed me that I had replied to one of her ads and she
was planning on opening a wellness center. After holding
many meetings and looking at spaces, she came up with
the name of her center: Flourish.

As I continued on my self-healing path, I came
across a business book that my best friend had given me
a couple years prior. I opened it up and read the message
she had written for me inside: "A small but powerful gift
that has immense potential to make your business and

life grow and flourish." When she had given me the book, I had no intention of starting my own business, so I just put it on the shelf. Two year later, the book and her message hit me like a ton of bricks. I was on the right path; this was it. Not only did the rediscovery of the book help me make my decision to join the Flourish Center, but it also came with tickets to a three-day business event that provided me with even more direction and confirmations.

I like to ask for signs. This may seem a little "woo-woo" to some, but many of my clients have incorporated this into their practice as well, and it works! I love butterflies, always have; they have incredible meaning. The butterfly is a symbol of change and powerful transformation. A secondary meaning of the butterfly is about finding joy in life and lightness of being. I ask to be shown butterflies when I am on the right path. These could be live butterflies in the appropriate seasons or pictures of butterflies. I use butterflies not only as a sign I am on the right path, but for anything.

One instance was when we traveled to the Dominican Republic for my sister-in-law's wedding and my son became very sick in the middle of the night. We ended up having to take him to the hospital there. My husband went with him in the ambulance, as I was uncomfortable going alone in an unfamiliar country and one of us had to stay with the rest of our children. After a few hours, and the reassurance from my husband that I would be safe and the hospital was a good one, I took a taxi to see my son and allow my husband to return to the resort to be with his family. As I was traveling in the taxi alone, I felt nervous, anxious and scared. I asked for a sign to show me that I was safe and that everything was going to be all right. I looked out the window, and there it was—a beautiful yellow butterfly fluttering in the grass alongside the roadway in the same direction I was going. I instantly felt peaceful, and my heart was warm. Every time I see a butterfly, I smile, knowing that I am on the right path.

Think of a symbol you really love, this could be an animal, a color, a shape, a flower. Decide that every time you see a daisy, for example, you'll know you're on the right path. Or if you're unsure about something, ask to see your symbol to determine whether that decision is right for you. One of my clients uses hearts. For her, hearts will appear as a cloud, and she will find heart-shaped rocks, and see heart reflections and pictures. Your symbol will bring confirmation that you're on the right path and honoring your self-love, as you will feel lightness and happiness each time you see it.

When you're open to opportunity and signs, big or small, your whole world opens up. Prior to my self-healing journey, I had blinders on. I was following the path that I felt everyone else would be happy seeing me on, feeding off their happiness and falsely claiming it as my own. Once I hit rock bottom and had my wake-up call, everything changed and I realized I was not being true to myself. Now when I tell people my story and they learn I was an electrician, they sometimes react with disbelief. "How could you possibly go from one extreme to the other?" they wonder. When you become aware of your feelings and what you really want, making the appropriate changes and sacrifices is a no-brainer. Deciding not to return to work as an electrician after I had my fourth child was simple; I knew in my heart it wasn't the path for me and I had to make a change. The clients I work with often share with me that they are thankful for my choice, as I have been able to assist them in greatly improving their lives. For that I am grateful, and it makes my heart so happy—yet another, but definitely not that last, confirmation that I am doing the right thing.

Here is another valuable exercise for you to do. On a day when you're feeling excited, your heart is singing and your self-love is at its peak, write an empowerment letter to yourself. Write about all the things you love about yourself, the direction you want to go and everything you're grateful for. Read this letter when a difficult situation arises that tests your self-worth and self-love. As you're reading, self-doubt or self-sabotage may arise. Take a huge breath and say to yourself, "That is not true, I am... (your empowering self-love sentence)." If you can do this while looking in a mirror, it will be even more powerful. When the tears come, let them come, and have a full release.

On your self-healing journey, there are going to be harder times. Do not relish them. Prepare yourself ahead of time with the exercises provided in this book, particularly your celebration journal, and your empowerment letter to yourself. These will remind you of all the good things and enable you to quickly switch back to a state of self-love—your happiness.

When something feels truly good to you, in your heart you are happy, and that alone is a confirmation of being on the right path or in the right place at the right time. This happiness is within you, pure and long-lasting; it is your self-love.

Tools to Discover Self-Love

- Second Mirror exercise—Look into your eyes in a mirror and tell yourself that you love you. Tell yourself the things you love about yourself.
- Integrity exercise
  - Complete what is unfinished.
- Ask for a sign.
- Write yourself an empowerment letter.

Previous Tools to Continue Using

- Do your best to read this book every day.
- Contribute daily to your celebration journal and review it right before bed.
- Set aside fifteen minutes minimum every day just for you.
- Feel your decisions.
- Turn "I can't" statements into "How can I?"
- Exchange negative thoughts for positive thoughts.
- Once a week, reflect on your motivational cue cards; replace as needed

- Doubt/Obstacle/Strategy exercise
- Limiting Belief vs. Empowering Belief exercise
- Keep saying, "No, thank you."
- Write in your release journal for twelve minutes a day for twelve days.
- Reflect, Release and Resolve
- Mirror exercise

Chapter 8

Listen Within

"The best day of your life is one which you decide your life is your own. No apologies or excuses. No one to lean on, rely on, or blame. The gift is yours—it is an amazing journey—and you alone are responsible for the quality of it. This is the day your life really begins."
—Bob Moawad, *author of* Whatever It Takes

Times will come when others do not agree with you or will give you conflicting advice. As you become more confident to trust in yourself and your choices, to listen within and make decisions that are right for you, you will be freed from heartache and the disapproval of others. You will feel free, weightless and unaffected by other people's opinions. Along with doubts, some opinions brought up by others are important to acknowledge, but do not dwell on them. With the exercises and advice in the previous chapters, this is becoming easier, as you are able to feel more connected to you, self-assured and confident, and more self-love and happiness from within yourself. You are not going to be able to make everyone happy, but you can most definitely make yourself happy. It is not selfish to take care of you first, to put your happiness first in the interest of self-healing and love. As a mom, this is a very important aspect of your journey. Please don't get me wrong. I'm not saying to neglect your children's needs but to allow yourself time each day for your needs, care and love also. Otherwise, you will be unable to genuinely assist or love another wholeheartedly. As a mom, you give and give and give to your children; you love them more than life itself, but without returning that love to yourself, you will find those tough times harder than they should be. This is the essential balance of giving and receiving. Give yourself the necessary time you deserve to rebalance and reground yourself each day. An analogy that I love to use as a visual for my clients is to imagine yourself as a tree. A tree that has a solid root system and is grounded deep and far within the earth will sway with the winds and storms, but a tree with a weak root system will be knocked down and fall. The roots are your investment in yourself, your self-care and your well-being. The journey you are on is for you; some people won't understand or agree with it, but that is because it is not their path, it's yours.

For the first portion of my life, I was on autopilot, just going through the motions and was not present with myself and others. It wasn't until I realized that I was on the wrong path and reconnected with myself that I started listening from within. I didn't know there was a difference from how I was living until I experienced the true connections with others through my heart and gave compassion and love wholeheartedly. One of my favorite moments on my journey of personal growth was when I truly and honestly felt the pure love and connection with my husband. I had always loved him, but when I reconnected with the love for myself, my love for him was able to expand to a level I had never imagined, a level that continues to grow and expand every day. My husband and I can now freely and openly speak our minds, and effectively communicate our concerns and feelings without fear. This was a huge step, because before, I would run away and avoid both his and my concerns. Starting my journey back to myself after six years of marriage, I gradually came to appreciate the patience he had with me for all those years. Initially, I felt extreme guilt for putting him through what I had, but once that was released, our connection was able to reseal and rapidly grow to an unimaginable level. As I progressed through discoveries, I would share them with him, as well as the areas where I needed assistance and support from him. I am grateful for these insights, and now we are able to enjoy each other and be completely open and honest.

Listening from within will become easier for you as time goes by. Once you have learned to listen to yourself, you will feel lighter and whole. You will view people and situations differently and be able to be more open to what they may be feeling or experiencing. Other people's reactions, judgments and actions will not affect you as they used to, as you now know they have nothing to do with you. All this happens very quickly once you're on the right path and able to listen from within. You will start to notice that situations that would have been very challenging for you in the past are now easier to deal with and flow by, rather than lingering and causing more difficulties. Different people will begin to show up in your life who are in alignment with you; some will become mentors and others will bring amazing lessons, discoveries and confirmations. Your relationships will become more authentic and purposeful.

It is essential to remain open to the challenging situations that will arise throughout your life. They can be an indication that you need to reconnect and listen from within, reflect on your practices and determine whether you have fallen away from doing any of them. It is easy to get comfortable and forget to maintain and continue practicing and taking time for you to do what you love. It is very common to start feeling good and decide to stop your self-healing journey, but in fact, this is the time to really focus and keep moving the process forward. Situations will arise that bring new discoveries to help you learn and grow. Being self-aware is incredibly valuable for your growth. When you are conscious, connected and open, you will know right away when something is off, and you will be able to adjust to reconnect with whatever you need at that time.

Trust how you're feeling within, follow your heart and open your mind to the possibilities. You may be surprised what can show up for you when you're in alignment with your heart and purpose. When your vision is clear and open to all possibilities, your life begins to flow effortlessly, giving small confirmations and gifts to continue on your current path. After some coaching, reminders and self-discovery, one of my clients came to know what she liked doing but didn't see it as feasible and viewed it as "maybe one day" it could be a career. She was searching for other options, but none of them worked out. One day she was approached by someone to do the very thing she liked doing! This was her confirmation. You will be surprised at the signs that appear and how much lines up for you once you listen from within and are open to all opportunities.

Tools to Listen Within

- Start noticing and being aware of your surroundings and the opportunities that begin to arise for you.
- Resolve issues from the past that are weighing you down or holding you back.

Previous Tools to Continue Using

- Do your best to read this book every day.
- Contribute daily to your celebration journal and review it right before bed.
- Set aside fifteen minutes minimum every day just for you.
- Feel your decisions.
- Turn "I can't" statements into "How can I?"
- Exchange negative thoughts for positive thoughts.
- Once a week, reflect on your motivational cue cards, replace as needed
- Doubt/Obstacle/Strategy exercise
- Limiting Belief vs. Empowering Belief exercise
- Write in your release journal for twelve minutes a day for twelve days.
- Keep saying, "No, thank you."

- Reflect, Release and Resolve
- Mirror exercises
- Integrity exercise
- Ask for a sign.

Chapter 9

Set Clear Intentions & Be Open

"It's not selfish to love yourself and to make your happiness a priority. It's necessary."
—*Mandy Hale, author of* The Single Woman

Your journey has been full of profound discoveries and changes that have led to so much personal growth. Just remember, personal development and growth is continuous throughout your life and will progressively deepen and advance. Great connection within, the ability to trust your heart in all decisions, and the beginning of incredible things are happening and appearing in your life. When you start to feel amazing within, it can be tempting to stop, but I encourage you to keep growing. Just when you think you're feeling better, keep going. Just when you feel it couldn't get any better, keep going. When you feel you are at the top, keep going. Continue to become more open to all that is presented in your life; embrace the signs, confirmations and guidance. Your life will be filled with discoveries, you will continue to grow throughout it, and as long as you continue to follow your heart, you will continue upwards in your own happiness.

At times you might feel like you're going back to your old patterns and habits, or things aren't coming together with ease and flow. These are times to reconnect and notice what has changed. Are you still honoring yourself every day? Are you staying true to yourself and doing what is right for you, and not what others want? Are you saying, "No, thank you" when a request doesn't suit you? Are you living a life of integrity? Are you still celebrating even the smallest of successes? Be self-aware and self-observant at all times to ensure you are being your authentic self.

Your mind is incredibly strong, now that you are connected within yourself and honoring what makes you feel good and your heart sing; you can manifest all that you want for your life. One of the strongest tools is to envision and feel what you want as if it is already happening. There are many great teachers for manifestation and using mantras to aid in the creation of what you desire. For as long as I can remember, into my childhood and growing up, all I ever wanted after high school was to get married and have a big family. I repeated that same desire my whole life, with an innocent intention. When I was eighteen I met my life partner, and when I was nineteen we got married and began our family right away. It happened! I didn't learn about this practice until I was twenty-seven, but I had already been putting it to work.

One of the first exercises of manifesting that I was shown was vision boarding. A vision board is a collection of words, phrases and pictures that represent your goals, intentions, wants, desires and dreams. This is a powerful exercise that can change your life and make what you desire really happen. Be as clear and specific as possible to ensure that you're indeed visioning exactly what you want. If you would like to travel, put specific destinations on the board. If you would like to travel with someone, be sure to include pictures of two people, two meals, two drink glasses. If it is a car that you desire, make sure you show the right color, year and model. Pick pictures that depict *exactly* what you would like. Place your board in a location where you will see it multiple times a day. Once you begin to accomplish different parts of your board, mark them off with a beautiful symbol to show they are complete. When you are connected with what you want, the decisions you make in your life begin to flow, and become freeing and easy, because you know the direction you are going, or at least desire to go. You will start meeting the right people at the right time and will be given opportunities that you've been waiting for that will allow you to grow and prosper.

When you are clear about your intentions, self-confident and connected, outside influence and opinions won't alter your choices. Judgment from self and others is also reduced and can no longer affect you. A lot of hurt and pain are eliminated when you become reconnected and find your self-love. There is no more working to please others and satisfy their needs, opinions and wants; it is now about you and being confident with your choices. In turn, when you're happy and your intentions are pure, it reflects in all your relationships. You will attract like-minded individuals, and you will begin to see who may not be supportive or necessary in your life anymore. People will either come along with you for the journey, or they will begin to weed themselves out naturally. A lot of the people who didn't support my initial desire to become a natural health practitioner really supported me as an electrician, but when I decided to go back into natural healing, they either came along with me or I was going along without them. Their opinion didn't weigh on my decision because I was confident within myself and knew what I needed to do. Every person who crosses your path has a purpose, whether it is for a discovery, for your growth or for your support. Embrace all who come into your life and accept what they bring; they are there for a reason.

A great exercise to help deepen your integrity and connect with yourself is making a list of your core values. Determining your core values will allow you to set clear intentions and be open to achieving what you want by using them as your guides. For example, you can compare values the people you hire: for example, a nanny, housekeeper or contractor.. Core values are the foundation of how you conduct yourself, what you live by daily and in every situation use to guide you. They make who you are. My core values are:

- Appreciation
- Compassion
- Gratitude
- Honesty
- Integrity
- Love

Below is a suggested list of values. First, go through the list and write down all the words that are meaningful to you. Then, go through this short list and pick out five to seven core values.

Abundance	Daring	Idealism	Reverence
Acceptance	Dedication	Imagination	Righteousness
Accomplishment	Dependability	Immovability	Sacrifice

Achievement	Detachment	Informative	Self-confidence
Action-oriented	Determination	Inclusiveness	Serenity
Adaptability	Devotion	Insight	Service
Adventure	Diligence	Integrity	Sharing
Affection	Dignity	Intelligence	Spirituality
Alertness	Diplomacy	Intimacy	Strength
Ambition	Direction	Intuition	Stability
Appreciation	Directness	Joy	Sturdiness
Ardent	Discernment	Justice	Support
Authenticity	Discretion	Kindness	Togetherness
Balance	Discipline	Knowledge	Toughness
Beauty	Discovery	Lasting	Trustworthiness
Belief	Diversity	Leadership	Truth
Beneficent	Contentment	Harmony	Peace
Benevolent	Courage	Happy	Performance
Bliss	Courtesy	Healing	Perseverance
Boldness	Creativity	Health	Persistence
Bravery	Cunning	Helpful	Personableness
Brilliance	Curiosity	Honesty	Planning
Briskness	Dreaming	Honorable	Politeness
Candid	Drive	Hope	Positive outlook
Care	Duty	Humanitarianism	Power
Carefulness	Durability	Humility	Professionalism
Certainty	Empathy	Humor	Prosperity
Challenge	Empowerment	Learning	Purity
Charity	Energetic	Legacy	Purpose
Charm	Enthusiastic	Love	Recognition
Chastity	Ethical	Loyalty	Resourcefulness
Cheerfulness	Equality	Malleability	Respect
Clarity	Excellence	Mastery	Responsibility
Classy	Faithfulness	Maturity	Understanding
Cleanliness	Fearless	Meaningful	Union
Cleverness	Finesse	Memorable	Unity
Commitment	Flexibility	Merciful	Valiant
Communication	Forgiveness	Neatness	Vigorous

Compassion	Formidable	Neighborly	Virtuous
Competence	Freedom	Nimble	Wisdom
Complacency	Free-thinking	Noble	Wonder
Completion	Fresh	Non-conforming	Yes-minded
Composure	Friendship	Nurturing	Youthfulness
Concentration	Fun	Obedience	Zen
Confidence	Gallant	Objectivity	
Conformity	Generosity	Openness	
Congruency	Gentleness	Opportunity	
Connection	Genuine	Optimism	
Credibility	Goodness	Organization	
Coherence	Goodwill	Originality	
Cooperation	Gratitude	Outstanding	
Confidence	Growth	Passion	
Connection	Harmlessness	Patience	

Finding my core values assisted me in connecting even deeper to how I wanted to conduct my life. Surrounding myself with people who have similar core values allowed me to make powerful connections that vastly improved my self-healing journey. I now have leading mentors, coaches and advisors in my life who have allowed my growth to escalate! The perfect situations continue to present themselves.

One guidance that I am so grateful for arose when I was feeling as though I had been in the same spot on my journey with my business and my clients for a while, so I put it out there to show me a sign and guide me where I needed to go. My husband had surprised me with arranging daycare for our kids so that we could go on a date. We hopped on our motorcycles and went on a ride up to a local ski resort, Sun Peaks, to have breakfast. I couldn't help but notice all the For Sale signs on our way up the hill. I mentioned this to my husband during breakfast and we decided to stop at a couple of them, just to explore. For the last couple of years, we had been talking about whether we should move from our current home because we were starting to outgrow it and it wasn't our ideal property.

When we got home that afternoon, I went online to check out a couple of the properties we had come across, just out of curiosity. I noticed at the top of the screen a heading that read, "New Listings in the Area." One in particular caught my eye, so I clicked and started investigating. WOW! It was absolutely perfect. We had made a list of the things we would like for our home, and this place had almost all of them. The power of manifestation at work. I contacted our realtor and we went to view the property the next day and instantly fell in love—it felt like home. The following day, we found out there was already an offer on the place, so without much discussion, we jumped and decided to put in an offer as well. We weren't quite sure how we were going to pull it off, as we couldn't sell our current house immediately. It was about a year away from being ready. I put our house online for rent to own to see if there would be any interest. It didn't take long for a beautiful family to view it and want it instantly. Somehow, everything came together and we got the new place! We moved in a short month later. We found out that the house had been for sale for more than a year, but the owners had just lowered the price. If that hadn't happened, I would never have seen the listing.

When you ask with clear intentions and remain open to all opportunities, you will receive all that you need.

Tools to Set Clear Intentions & Be Open

- Create a vision board to start manifesting exactly what you would like to show up in your life.
- List your core values and then focus in on them to deepen your integrity and connection within yourself.

Previous Tools to Continue Using

- Do your best to read this book every day.
- Contribute daily to your celebration journal and review it right before bed.

- Set aside fifteen minutes minimum every day just for you.
- Feel your decisions.
- Turn "I can't" statements into "How can I?"
- Exchange negative thoughts for positive thoughts.
- Once a week, reflect on your motivational cue cards, replace as needed
- Doubt/Obstacle/Strategy exercise
- Limiting Belief vs. Empowering Belief exercise
- Write in your release journal as needed.
- Keep saying, "No, thank you."
- Reflect, Release and Resolve
- Mirror exercises
- Integrity exercise
- Ask for a sign.
- Notice new opportunities.
- Make amends.

Chapter 10

Live It

"Let today be the day you finally release yourself from the imprisonment of past grudges & anger. Simplify your life. Let go of the poisonous past & live the abundantly beautiful present... today."
—*Steve Maraboli, bestselling author* Life, the Truth, and Being Free

Look at how amazing you're doing! I'm so excited for you to be at this point in your journey. You have connected so many dots on your path, and I know the motivation has kicked into full gear to allow you to pursue what makes you happy and your heart sing. You are living it!

Have you started noticing things showing up in your life that are confirming the direction you're going? Guidance that allows you to easily take your next step? It feels amazing, doesn't it? If you haven't, ask for a sign for direction, keep putting your intentions out, and be open to what you receive.

A challenge that can arise and is important to be aware of is not giving yourself away and not being open to receiving the amazing gifts from others. The balance of giving and receiving is so incredibly necessary to your growth, because it will allow you to accomplish and exceed your intentions. Before you give, ensure that you have taken the time to care for yourself, so that you can give wholeheartedly and without any expectations of receiving something in return. The universe works in surprising ways, and you will receive in different ways and possibly from different people, perhaps even people you have never given to before. Being open to receiving is an incredible gift that many people struggle with.

Prior to embarking on my self-healing journey, I would give, give, give and have huge hesitation about receiving anything in return. I loved giving gifts and doing things for my friends, family, clients and sometimes strangers, but if someone ever wanted to give to me or do something for me, it was very awkward and hard for me to accept. Similarly it was so hard for me to accept money for my services that instead of saying how much they cost, I would often give them away for free! Valuing yourself and allow yourself to receive gifts from others. These gifts can be powerful teachings, assistance or offerings that are beneficial to your personal development. Gifts don't always have a return value on them and don't have to. Be neutral and open.

From another perspective, I love giving, but I had to learn that not everyone will accept what I have to offer, because of personal beliefs or because they struggle to accept things from others. I also had to learn that it is okay when people do not accept what you're offering, and not to take it personally. You cannot push or force; people must learn their own lessons in their own time, if they choose to. For me, when someone does accept an offering or gift, it feels like receiving for me as well. It is an amazing gift to be able to give to someone else.

As you start pursuing your passions and dreams, there will be times of rejection, doubt and discovery; embrace them all as part of your journey. Celebrate all the acceptance and support you receive along the way. The most important thing is to follow your passion, whether it be sharing yourself with others, assisting others out of darkness or being with your children and bringing love and happiness into their lives, among many other possibilities. It could be finally doing what you always wanted with your life. Your journey could be the story that saves a life, if not many lives.

Whatever you put your mind to, you will accomplish. Don't let anyone tell you that you can't; in fact, allow that resistance to make you stronger and give you an extra boost to succeed. When I first started school to become a natural health practitioner, I was extremely excited and it felt so right. Because I was happy with what I was doing, my good marks came easily, I absorbed the information effortlessly and the process was really enjoyable. If I had been connected within myself at that time, I would have known that I was doing the right thing, and no one would have been able to change my mind. However, I let people around me influence me. Instead of staying true to myself and doing what made me happy, I changed my path to suit what satisfied the people around me. I am extremely grateful that I completed the training and received my diploma as a natural health practitioner before starting a new career, as this granted me the ability to do what I'm doing today. Use your vision board and motivational cards around your house to inspire you to do the things that you love every day.

Every situation that arises in your life happens for a reason. Becoming an electrician did serve a purpose at that time in my life. The income allowed my husband and I to have four beautiful children. It allowed me to experience hitting rock bottom by living a life that was not in alignment with my purpose, learning new things about myself and overcoming all of the challenges that came with finding myself again. There were a lot of difficult decisions I had to make and conflicts I had to face, and I finally had to put my foot down and say, "No, thank you" when it was necessary. These were all invaluable lessons that I needed to learn to live an extremely happy, freeing and purposeful life. They have allowed me to get to where I am today, to serve my purpose and assist others like you in finding themselves again and staying true to their path. The enlightenment to begin my journey to finding my way back to me was one of the greatest gifts I ever received.

Reflect on some of the things that have happened in your life. What benefit or discovery did they bring you? Sometimes it is very healing to turn a negative or unpleasant experience into something that moved you forward, made you stronger or allowed you to turn your life towards what you now love. For this, use the Pain to Positive exercise by drawing a two-column chart. In the first column, write one negative point about the experience. In the second column, write three to five good things that came out of that situation: the personal lessons, discoveries and growth. For example, if missed an appointment, write it down in the pain column. In the positive column, write down at least three good things that came out of it: you had more time for you, you got more errands done, you bumped into a friend you hadn't seen in awhile. If this brings up emotions, let them come, but focus on the quantity and quality of the good points and feel those with your heart.

I had a client whose dad left when she was really young. This caused her a lot of pain, but after focusing on the good that came out of the situation, she was able to see that she is a very independent and strong woman who learned that opportunities arose for her that may not have if he had stayed. If you have struggled with a deep wound, it may be beneficial for you to seek out a professional counselor who is a good fit for you. With your newfound self-love, you can move past the hurt and no longer allow it to control your life and your happiness. I am sending you so much love and support.

It can be difficult at times, but staying true to yourself, living your dream and leading a purposeful life is the most rewarding journey. That is truly "living it." Challenges are only bumps in the road to make you stronger and move you to that next step on your path. Now that you see that you are here for a reason, with amazing gifts to offer, you will live a happier, freer and more prosperous life.

At this point, you are far into your journey of self-healing and personal development, and progressing forward in a beautiful and connected manner. Unless you let yourself fall back into old habits, you will continue to blossom and move forward happily. There may be times when you do stray off your path, but you will receive nuggets of information and opportunities to get you back on course. Remember, you're the only one in control of your happiness; no one can take it away from you, unless you let them. Living the life that lights you up, that makes you appreciative and grateful, is living it.

I love taking the time for myself, and I do, but for me being a mom and the work I do are my passions, so everything I do is something I love! I have always said I wanted the best of both worlds: the balance between being a mom and working at something I love. I am living it—my purpose and passion—which results in self-satisfaction and utmost happiness. This is what I hope you will find, through the tools and techniques of this book, combined with the discoveries and growth opportunities that life has to offer you.

Tools to Live It

- Start receiving gifts from others with open arms and a heartfelt "Thank you."
- Us the Pain to Positive exercise to turn negative or unpleasant situations into constructive attributes.
- Seek professional support when necessary.

Previous Tools to Continue Using

- Do your best to read this book every day.
- Contribute daily to your celebration journal and review it right before bed.
- Set aside fifteen minutes minimum every day just for you.
- Feel your decisions.
- Turn "I can't" statements into "How can I?"
- Exchange negative thoughts for positive thoughts.
- Once a week, reflect on your motivational cue cards, replace as needed
- Doubt/Obstacle/Strategy exercise
- Limiting Belief vs. Empowering Belief exercise
- Write in your release journal as needed.
- Keep saying, "No, thank you."
- Reflect, Release and Resolve
- Mirror exercises
- Integrity exercise
- Ask for a sign.
- Notice new opportunities.
- Make amends.
- Create a vision board.
- List your core values.

Afterword

Happy in Love with You Again

Congratulations on making it to the end of this book! You have made a huge accomplishment, and you should celebrate!

Now you should be feeling lighter and seeing things more clearly, and those little things that used to really get under your skin, don't anymore. You are able to stop the negative thoughts at the top of the tornado, recollect yourself and move forward. You have released past emotions and issues that were holding you back. You have found yourself again and connected to your heart and what makes you happy. You have found your purpose, which has led you to your passions, or you are well on your way to clarifying it. What an incredible gift you have given yourself. A gift that will keep growing and growing, not only for you but for everyone in your life, now and in the future. You will now have a positive ripple effect; your determination, love and passion will extend to everyone around you, and then reach even further as they're passed along. Your children will follow your example to learn these tools and techniques and use them to grow and guide themselves to live a life filled with happiness and self-awareness. You will be able to assist them in challenging times, ones that will build them up instead of break them down.

Your journey of self-love is not over; it has just begun and will continue to advance. You have completed the hardest part, and now it is very important to sustain it. I recommend continuing to honor yourself with a minimum of fifteen minutes per day to do something for you and with just you. Although maintaining your self-love is quite simple, it can be easy to fall away from. When you feel like you've reached your peak, when you're feeling connected, free and living with ease, it is tempting to stop your "you" time. If you do, you will start to get little signs here and there—frustration, anger, feelings of detachment, the sense that things aren't lining up as well as they used to—that will give you the clear indication that you need to reconnect. Let this be a symbol to take extra time for you. This will be easy for you, as you have all the tools you need, you know what you love and what makes your heart happy, it is just a matter of allotting that time to honor yourself daily. Know that you always have this book to refer to. If you read it using a highlighter, and then reread it, you will see just how much has improved for you over time and the new discoveries you've made. This can be a nice reminder of how far you've come.

Your journey has made you who you are today. I believe we are all here to serve others and work together to make a difference, not only for ourselves and others but for the whole world. You have overcome many challenges, learned many lessons and weathered many failures, which have resulted in discoveries and personal growth. Turning your perspective around to see these as positive opportunities has uplifted you and built you up, instead of tearing you down and breaking you apart. Let them make you stronger instead of limiting you. This will change your life. If it feels right to you, sharing your discoveries with others who are open to it can not only assist them, allowing them to change their perspective and their lives. In turn, they may go on to share their experience, and the ripple effect will carry on. To benefit others is a true gift, and knowing that you are able to do just that by sharing your journey is rewarding and confirming. Some of the discoveries you have made could be for the benefit of many, whereas others may be for your children, your partner, your best friend. From one to many, every positive change is rewarding for the soul.

There is no such thing as a straight path of motherhood. It is not easy, it isn't perfect and it is a process filled with discoveries and learning. There are perfect and easy times, but often it takes some discoveries to get there. Life is full of ups and downs, tests and triumphs, mistakes and learning. And life is full of discoveries. It is all in the eye of the beholder. With the knowledge you have gained, the personal growth you have experienced and the gifts you have given yourself, you are ready to live happily in love with you again. This is the greatest accomplishment you can achieve for yourself. Let your passion drive you to greatness. Continue to honor yourself every day, as this is the greatest gift you can give yourself and everyone in your life, especially the ones closest to you. This journey is for you first; start at the roots and your tree will grow to flourish, blossom and sway with ease as the discoveries of life emerge.

Gratitude & Appreciation

I would like to acknowledge Shirarose Wilensky, who assisted me with editing *The Busy Mom's Greatest Companion*. Shirarose, you made the process easy as you guided me through transforming my original jumbled manuscript into a book! I couldn't have done it without you and I'm so grateful for your expertise.

To my husband, Owen Munson, you have stood by me through thick and thin on this insane journey. Thank you for being my shoulder to cry on, my constant, and for supporting me through some of the toughest moments of my life. I appreciate you more than words can express.

My best friends, Jasmin Schenk and Nicole Kun, who have believed in me from the start, even when I didn't believe in myself. Thank you for pushing me, for your encouragement, and your support to keep going.

For my amazing mentors, who have guided me through and who have made a huge impact on different parts of this journey. Leanne Oaten, Brant Hasanen, Isabelle Hamptonstone, Cindy Piva, Yolanda Dye and Colin Sprake, I'm am forever grateful.

About the Author

Tracy Munson's goal is for all moms to think of themselves as extraordinary! She is the founder of Insight Natural Healing and The Overwhelmed Mom platform. She is a natural health strategist and coach with a natural health practitioner's diploma and is a certified Dream Coach®. With comprehensive training and experience, she specializes in working with overwhelmed moms with young kids to restore their calm and happiness, even through the busyness of life. She has a broad understanding and is experienced in working with young women and moms as they progress through different life stages. Her compassion, empathy and open mind allow people to feel completely comfortable and supported through their journey.

Tracy lives near Sun Peaks, in British Columbia, Canada, with her husband and four young children.